The Dwindling Probability of Solving the UFO Enigma

Jordan Hofer and David Barker

4880 Lower Valley Road • Atglen, PA 19310

Other Schiffer Books by the Authors:

Evolutionary UFOlogy. ISBN: 978-0-7643-4505-0

Little Gray Bastards: The Incessant Alien Presence. ISBN: 978-0-7643-5005-4

Other Schiffer Books on Related Subjects:

A Silent Invasion: The Truth About Aliens, Alien Abductions, and UFOs.
Reverend Debra Marshall. ISBN: 978-0-7643-4609-5

The Essential Guide to UFO Sightings Since 1945. Frank Schwede. ISBN: 978-0-7643-5437-3

Library of Congress Control Number: 2017935605

Cover design by Matt Goodman
Cover Illustration and original cover design concept © 2016 Mark Madland

Jordan Hofer Author's Photo © 2016 Mark Madland
David Barker Author's Photo © 2016 Judy Barker

Type set in ITC Benguiat Std/Times New Roman

ISBN: 978-0-7643-5423-6
Printed in the United States of America

Published by Schiffer Publishing, Ltd.
4880 Lower Valley Road
Atglen, PA 19310
Phone: (610) 593-1777; Fax: (610) 593-2002
E-mail: Info@schifferbooks.com
Web: www.schifferbooks.com

Jordan

To Shreya Joshi and the next generation of ufologists. May your investigations reveal more fruitful answers than my own.

David

To my dear wife, Judy, and our four wonderful daughters, for all the love and support you have given me over the years; and for our late dog, Franny, who spent many a sunny afternoon in the backyard with me, dozing in the ivy while I did my research reading for this book.

I don't doubt that there's life out there at all. I think there's probably been some alien contact on Earth. But after talking to a bunch of ufologists here, I think that 99.9% of people who are out there, being the most vocal, are really doing a disservice to the truth. They play with facts. Some of them are hoaxers. They need to use the same sort of rigor that the skeptics are asking them to use and then maybe we'll get to the truth. I should say that on the other side of the equation the skeptics need to get the giant skeptic's d— out of their a— and allow themselves to respect the people who have made these claims. I think they need to work together. That's how we're going to find out whether aliens exist.

— Casey Feldman
The Real 'X-Files'?
VICE Network: December 4, 2015

Contents

Foreword

One night a few years ago, my wife and I were walking along the beach near our home in Massachusetts. It was dusk; there was a storm out to sea, and the waves were gigantic.

This beach is on a barrier island. Beyond the sizable sand dunes are miles of sea marsh that stretch out in almost every direction.

We were watching these huge waves crash against the shore when something caught my eye over the marshes to the south. It was a group of lights—white, amber, and red—blinking furiously and flying not fifty feet above the marshland. They were heading right for us.

Before I could say anything to my wife, a second set of lights—exact same colors and same frenzied blink rate—appeared, flying beside the first. When I finally pointed them out to her, they were about a half-mile away and still coming right at us.

I blurted out: "Oh my God—I'm finally going to see a UFO . . ."

Everything we were seeing fit the criteria of a typical UFO sighting. Unusually blinking aerial lights, lack of sound, atypical flying characteristics (these things could not be airplanes; they were flying too low and too fast).

We stopped in our tracks. The lights were very bright now and almost on top of us. I remember her saying: "I can't believe this . . ."

Then the lights went over our heads, and we saw what they really were: two Medivac helicopters, flying side-by-side, carrying two patients to a nearby hospital. I was hugely disappointed.

I've loved reading about UFOs all my life and have even written books about them. Yet I've never seen one. And if the evidence brought out in *Unidentifiable Flying Objects: The Dwindling Probability of Solving the UFO Enigma* is valid, the chances of me ever seeing a real UFO are rapidly diminishing.

I agree with the authors that a lot of what's out there concerning UFOs—in books, podcasts, radio shows, and on TV—is total BS. I believe ninety percent of it is just interference that distracts from the ten percent that might actually be something strange or unearthly happening.

But as my own personal experience points out, the skies are becoming very crowded these days. Between commercial aircraft, private aircraft, military aircraft, and suddenly thousands of drones flying around, it's getting increasingly difficult to have a "typical" UFO sighting. Everything else just keeps getting in the way.

In these pages, Jordan and David make this case in spades. The fewer credible sightings of UFOs these days—not just by hoaxers and hucksters, but by sincere people who just happen to be seeing strangely acting helicopters blinking a wide array of lights—the less information UFO researchers will have to work with in the future, keeping us that much further away from discovering the truth about these strange objects that have been seen in Earth's skies for thousands of years.

Luckily we have with this book, a well–researched, clearly written dissertation on the problem. I urge all readers to listen to what the authors are trying to tell us. These days, and in the days to come, we have to display a healthy dose of doubt when it comes to the UFO puzzle. Doubt what we hear, what we're told, and what we see. Seek out only those UFO events that have multiple witnesses, credible photography, and are able to discount any other earthly explanation for what was seen.

As the authors conclude: when it comes to questionable UFO evidence, don't be afraid to say: "I don't know."

—Mack Maloney

Author of *UFOs During Wartime*
and radio host of
Mack Maloney's Military X-Files

Acknowledgments

Thank you to Tracie Austin, Judy Barker, Hayley Barker, Molly Barker, Taryn Barker, Tessa Barker, Dan Barker, Chris Barker, Tom Bowden, William Carpenter, Pat Daniels, Peter Davenport, Mellie Devault, Mel Fabregas, David Halperin, Jim Harold, Kellie Haulotte, Mallory Heart, Anna Hofer, John Hofer, Jeffrey Huey, Dr. David M. Jacobs, Shreya Joshi, Douglas Hogate Jr., Jennabee Hogate Keen, Ed Komarek, Dr. Rita Louise, Mark and Jennifer Madland, Mack Maloney, Kathleen Marden, Linda Olsenius and Chris Olsenius, Nick Pope, Rick Prewitt, Paul Dale Roberts, Alejandro Rojas, Dinah Roseberry, Keith Rowell, Corina Saebels, Pete Schiffer, Dave Schrader, Reverend Tim Shaw, Brad Steiger, Denise Stoner, Lady Selah SuJuris, Kate Valentine, Michael Vara, Brett Watson, Kevin Wierzbicki, Butch Witkowski, and Bryce Zabel. Apologies to anyone missed.

PREFACE

Travis Walton Falls Down

> Extraordinary evidence requires extraordinary claims.
>
> —Jordan Hofer
>
> (In response to Carl Sagan's dictum concerning UFOs)

The annual UFO Festival in McMinnville, Oregon (a.k.a. "Saucerville") is held every May and is the second largest such event in the United States, topped only by the July festivities in Roswell, New Mexico. Saucerville's festival commemorates the Trent sighting of May 11, 1950, and the two exceptional photos of a saucer-shaped craft that flew over the Trents' family farm, snapped by Paul Trent with his Kodak Roamer camera. The photos have never been debunked and remain two of the most convincing pieces of photographic evidence of a flying saucer ever captured. The UFO festival celebrates its nineteenth year in 2018.

On the evening of May 14, 2015, at approximately 8:00 p.m., special guest speaker Travis Walton was fielding questions from the audience. He said that his general health had only grown more robust after his five-day abduction in November 1975, and intimated that the aliens had something to do with his exceptional fitness. Then, literally moments later, Travis Walton fell down. As his strong, tall frame crumpled in free fall like a marionette with its strings cut, he hit the stage face first with the full force of his weight. My first thought was: *They got him.* Someone called 911. Thankfully, Travis rose to his feet amidst applause, and was led away to awaiting EMTs. The look in his eyes was of uncomfortable surprise.

Whatever happened to Walton on that spring evening in 2015, is anyone's guess. But I was there and saw it happen. Perhaps he was exhausted by his trip from Arizona. Maybe he was dehydrated, even though he was sipping from a bottle of water as he gave his presentation. Low blood sugar is another possibility. None of these is necessarily associated with poor health. So there was something uncanny and ironic about Travis Walton's fall—it had all the drama of a choreographed demonstration. Did *They* really get him? It sure as hell looked like it.

INTRODUCTION

Drones, CGI, and the Future of UFO Sightings in the Twenty-First Century

(by Jordan)

> The truth, of course, is that a billion falsehoods told a billion times by a billion people are still false.
>
> —Travis Walton

Ufology is running out of time in its quest to discover the truth about UFOs. First, forget the aliens—they're all fake, whether clever costume, puppetry, or subpar computer graphics. You can throw out all of the blurry lights caught on camera, too. Bright dots might be UFOs but they're almost ubiquitously boring and usually cannot be analyzed. Photographs and video of structured craft are rare and most of the recent ones are CGI hoaxes.

Now there are thousands of drones, large and small, about 10,000 registered in Oregon alone according to a local R/C hobby dealer. FAA.gov designates three categories of drone:

1. Public Operations (Governmental)
2. Civil Operations (Non-governmental)
3. Model Aircraft (Hobby or recreation *only*)

According to *USA Today* (February 8, 2016) 325,000 people recently completed registration for private drones; I assume this number represents both Civil Operations and Model Aircraft categories. Further, 325,000 people may each own at least more than one drone, and others several, so that the total number of private drones may well be 750,000 to a million. I cannot find any definite numbers for Public Operations (Governmental) drones. However, I did discover that not only the US Air Force owns and operates these drones but other governmental agencies as well, including the CIA, FBI, Department of Homeland Security, and various police departments across the country (*The Atlantic*, March 10, 2016).

So now well more than a million drones operate in United States airspace (actually, *millions* now). Some you can hold in the palm of your hand while others require a runway. And here is where ufology is really screwed: Some of these drones are enhanced by hobbyists and designed to appear *exactly* like UFOs.

UFO reporting centers, like MUFON's online reporting system and Peter Davenport's NUFORC, will be flooded with photographs of brightly lit objects and video of those objects performing "impossible" aerial maneuvers. With all the noise, the signal of *real* UFOs could be drowned in static.

But as a good friend pointed out, these difficulties need to be countered with a sharp eye for the solid cases: multiple credible witnesses, clear photographs, and video that can be analyzed. The CGI and drone problems force the researcher to consider only the very best evidence and to be vigilant against bullshit. This is not a simple mandate, for the mind is ripe to produce bullshit.

Recently some friends and I went on a "UFO hunt" in an area we knew was recently a hotbed of UFO activity. The driver stopped the car on a promontory and we all scanned the sky. Suddenly we spotted a bright light hovering over the horizon.

"It's moving!" one of us exclaimed.

"You're right," said another. "From side to side."

"Up and down," I added.

"To the right!"

"To the left!"

"Up!"

"Down!"

We quickly realized that our detection of motion was not consistent between the three of us. Meanwhile, the fourth was aiming his phone at the object and calling up an astronomy app. "Guys," he said.

"It moved again!" one of us said.

"No, it didn't," said the man with the phone. "It's Jupiter."

I felt crestfallen and a bit the fool. We wanted to see a UFO so badly that we were misinterpreting the motion of our eyes for that of Jupiter! Be vigilant against your own bullshit.

I have been studying ufology for seven years now and I still have not seen a UFO. I do not perceive this as an indication that UFOs do not exist but as a personal feeling of exclusion and frustration from not seeing what so many around me have witnessed. How many books must I write before I get to see a UFO?

And here is another confounding variable in my research: I am further from understanding the UFO phenomenon now than I was when I began seven years ago!

In this book you will find frustration, consternation, and exasperation. The book is a catalog of failures even when the answers appear to be right before our eyes.

Yet the investigation continues . . .

The original cast of *Stranger Things*, from left to right: Jordan Hofer, Mark Madland, Micah Murphy. Even in our youth we looked up and were . . . confused. *Photograph by Jana Hofer, 1983.*

Aloha, David . . . UFO or Drone?

(David Barker's Comments)

On a balmy evening in September 2015, I was with my wife and one of our daughters attending the Chief's Luau at Sea Life Park on the Windward Coast of Oahu. We were seated at a picnic table, enjoying our meal, sipping drinks, and watching the Polynesian fire dancers on a nearby stage when my attention was drawn to an odd green light that was bobbing up and down in the sky above the cliffs behind us. Excited by the thought that I might be seeing a UFO, I ignored the show for fifteen minutes while I took dozens of photos of the unusual light with my cell phone. After a while, it dawned on me that the object kept rising from and returning to the exact same point on the cliff, and that it never once strayed very far from that location. Furthermore, its movements were slow and within the performance range of a typical consumer grade drone. Its appearance and behavior displayed none of the fantastic characteristics of a true UFO.

As the device continued to put on its own show in competition with the stage show, I reviewed my photos, decided they showed nothing more than a meaningless point of light, and deleted them. I'd been fooled by some hobbyist's toy into thinking I was seeing a UFO. No doubt, this same scenario is being played out continuously all over the world. The proliferation of low-cost drones have made it that much easier for skeptics to explain away UFO reports. Which means that as time goes by, witnesses will be even less likely to report unusual aerial objects than they are now, knowing they will only be ridiculed or, at best, told they are mistaken, and thus the odds of ever solving the UFO mystery will be further diminished.

Nonetheless, true UFO sightings are still possible in this drone-infested world. Early in the evening of February 16, 2016, I was outside my home in Salem, Oregon, placing some materials in the recycling bin when I happened to glance up at the sky to the east. There, about a mile away, at low elevation above a row of trees, was a long cigar-shaped object moving from south to north, which was my right to left. The object was perhaps one hundred feet long, a dull black or dark gray color, and had a row of four or more pale red lights evenly spaced along its length. No wings, cabin, or other details were visible, nor were there any other lights such as would be seen on a conventional aircraft. Three or four smaller white lights were hovering nearby, as if accompanying the craft. I could hardly believe my eyes, and it took me several seconds to admit to myself that I was seeing a UFO. The object moved quite slowly—slower than a typical airplane—and I realized I might be able to get a photo of it if I acted quickly. Grabbing my cell phone, I opened the camera program, allowed it to focus on the object, and pushed the camera icon to snap a photo, but then a strange thing happened. Each time I pushed the camera icon, the program flipped into self-portrait mode, and took a photo of my face instead of the object. Try as I might, the phone would not take a photo of the UFO, which was maddening. Frustrated, I gave up and went back to watching the object, which by now had moved a short distance to my left. After several seconds of watching it, I again tried to photograph it, with the same results, and gave up a second time. As I watched it once more for a few seconds, it didn't fly off but simply disappeared along with the accompanying white lights.

The total event lasted about one minute, roughly half of which I wasted trying to take photographs instead of looking at the objects. During the sighting, the cigar-shaped object disappeared and reappeared a couple of times. I didn't pay much attention to what the white lights were doing. The total relative distance traveled by the cigar-shaped object was the width of my hand held out at arm's length.

Oddly enough, I didn't give this sighting much thought until the next day when I finally looked at the photos to see if by pure luck I'd gotten any decent shots of the UFOs. What I had was a bunch of black frames with no images on them whatsoever, and three very dark photos of my face, with tiny highlights—apparently the UFOs—reflecting off the lenses of my glasses. The lights are so small and blurry they are useless as representations of what I had seen that night. The time stamp on my photos was 7:06 p.m.

Why was I unable to capture a single good photo of this event? Maybe I was so excited that I was pushing the wrong icons on the screen of my cell phone, and making it flip into "selfie" mode myself. This is not too likely, however, as the self-portrait icon on my phone is at the top of the screen and the camera icon used to take photos is at the bottom. A more ominous explanation occurs to me. There are many reports of aliens as well as paranormal entities affecting the behavior of electronic devices as a way to interact with humans. Did the occupants of the craft interfere with the operation of my cell phone? Were they, in effect, messing with me, spoiling the photos I was trying to take and instead—ironically—showing me only my own pathetically limited human face as I stared into the night at their mysterious display? Were they sending a message that when we think we are seeing them, what we're really seeing is ourselves? Did they play a trick on me and laugh in my face? Like most UFO witnesses, I'll never get an answer to my questions.

CHAPTER 1

CHAPTER 1

Introducing Shreya Joshi

(by Jordan)

"Set thy heart upon thy work, but never on its reward."

—Krishna-Dwaipayana Vyasa

The Bhagavad Gita

Ms. Shreya Joshi, ufologist for the Indian Paranormal Team.
Photograph by Sayan Sarkar, 2016.

Shreya Joshi is a twenty-one-year-old college student in chemistry. She is also the leading ufologist with the Indian Paranormal Team (http://indianparanormalteam.com/). I have had the pleasure of conversing with her and even working with her on a particularly frustrating case reviewed at the end of this chapter following the conversation section. I present our IM (instant message) dialogues unedited so her charming character is revealed to you.

May 7, 9:51 p.m.

Shreya Joshi: **SJ**
Jordan Hofer: **JH**
David Barker: **DB**

SJ: Thank you very much sir for accepting my friend request.
JH: Thanks for sending it.
SJ: Sir, I would like to learn on UFOs from you.
JH: Sure, Shreya. That's what we all try to do—keep each other informed.
SJ: That's really great.
JH: I'm a research specialist with the Mutual UFO Network (MUFON), a worldwide organization.
SJ: Wooaah! I'm very glad talking to you and sharing my thoughts with you.
JH: Me, too. Whatever you're thinking, studying, I'm interested.
SJ: I'm from India actually, and India very conservative to such topics.
JH: Well, UFOs are not exactly a subject that everyone is comfortable with. It's about 50/50 here in the US.
SJ: Here no one believes on such things; hardly any one believes. So, it's very difficult to prove such things to people, but still I'm trying to prove them all.
JH: I have found that you can't really prove it to people. They either accept the evidence or they don't.
SJ: Yes sir, you said right.
JH: My best friend of over 35 years saw a triangle UFO and then my daughter saw a red rectangle UFO. I HAD to accept the evidence! What about the theory of evolution? Is that accepted in India?
SJ: No!
JH: Same here. More people believe in UFOs than accept evolution.
SJ: Yes.
JH: So, do people in India generally believe Hinduism and that's it?
SJ: Yes, they only believe Hinduism.
JH: Interesting. The same is true here. Most people only believe in Christianity. I do like Hanuman. And the Ramayana is an incredible book!
SJ: Good to hear this from you that you like god Hanuman and the holy book Ramayana.
JH: As a university teacher I was introduced to many beliefs.
SJ: That's nice.
JH: I taught Christians, Hindus, Jews, Muslims, Buddhists, atheists . . . and I learned from them. Are you a student?

SJ: Yes sir. I'm doing Bachelor of Science in Chemistry.

JH: Oh, good for you! That is an area of study that will do well for you. My cousin is working on his PhD in biochemistry. Many of my family are scientists.

SJ: That's amazing. I'm also gonna do PhD in chemistry.

JH: You will definitely have a rewarding career.

SJ: Thank you sir!

JH: Do you like university?

SJ: Yes, of course!

JH: Good attitude! Do you know what you want to do as a chemist?

SJ: No sir, I don't know. Sir, you please suggest me what should I do.

JH: Shreya, you are so polite! You do not have to call me "sir."

SJ: No, you're elder than me I should respect you.

JH: Oh, I do appreciate that. If you're more comfortable with "sir," then that's okay. I suggest that you work hard and get your PhD in chemistry. After that, go into research, but not for a private company. In private companies, money always comes before data. You may find yourself in a position to choose between money and your integrity as a scientist. Aside from that, it sounds like you are a very intelligent young woman, and you will have a lot of options to choose from.

SJ: Yes sir, you're absolutely right and thank you very much for suggesting me. If I will have any doubts or confusion regarding this topic, I'll ask you before taking any step.

JH: Just stay honest and hardworking.

SJ: And yes, I will work hard to achieve my goal.

JH: Do you like living in India? Do you get to see your parents often?

SJ: Yes! I like to live in India after all it's my birthplace. Yes, I stay with them.

May 10, 9:55 a.m.

SJ: Hello sir!

JH: Hi Shreya!

SJ: How are you sir?

JH: Well today, Shreya. How was your trip?

SJ: It was awesome sir!

JH: What did you do?

SJ: I met my team's founder. I learnt tarot cards and healing from them.

JH: Very cool.

SJ: Yes sir.

JH: I used tarot cards in the past to help a friend who was addicted to drugs.

SJ: Oh! Nice. You always use to help everyone. This quality of yours I like in you sir. Sir, I have some confusion related to NIBIRU.

JH: Ah, Nibiru. As far as I can tell, it's nonsense.

SJ: Exactly sir, even I feel the same.

JH: Astronomers have said Nibiru does not exist.

SJ: But I thought to ask you about it whether it's all nonsense or not because you know more than me.

JH: I have been studying UFOs for 6 years now. It just gets weirder and weirder. Like The *X-Files*!

SJ: Yes sir! I went through the Google and searched on it but I saw someone was posting photos of Nibiru. So I thought to ask you. I have started researching on UFOs since a year only.

JH: The problem with photos these days is that computer graphics have gotten so good it's hard to tell the difference between what is real and what is not.

SJ: Yes sir, nowadays everyone do Photoshop and because of this it's too difficult to tell the difference between them.

May 14, 9:52 a.m.

SJ: Hello sir! Can you send me a very good link on evolution of human origin? Please!

JH: Yes, of course. I think Jared Diamond has done some great work. His books are standard reading. Here is his website: http://www.jareddiamond.org/Jared_Diamond/Welcome.html

SJ: Thank you so very much sir!

JH: My pleasure, Shreya!

May 20, 11:10 a.m.

SJ: Hello sir! How are you? I want to tell you something about my recent post.

JH: Please do so.

SJ: Sir, as you know I'm working in a team named Indian Paranormal Team and the Times Of India is very well known or very good newspaper in India. So I'm saying that yesterday my name and as well as my team's founders and members were mentioned in the newspaper for me. It's a good news as my name was never mentioned before in a newspaper like this so, I thought that I should let you know about this. I know it's hard to read what's written in the picture as the picture isn't clear, but if I will get the link of that headline then I'll send you the link for sure.

JH: That's great news, Shreya!

SJ: Thank you so much sir. By the way sir, I'm writing one article on "Founding of America".

JH: Interesting. Be sure to include how the European colonists killed almost all of the native people on this continent.

SJ: Sure sir!

June 3, 11:31 a.m.

SJ: Sir, dolphins are alien beings, is that true?

JH: Hi, Shreya. No, dolphins are not alien to this planet. They are related very closely to the toothed whales, all of which evolved from a land ancestor over 50 million years ago. Their closest living land relative today is the hippopotamus.

SJ: Oh! Actually I read somewhere that dolphins are alien beings, and I thought to ask you about it and you cleared my doubt very nicely. Thank you again!

JH: There is a lot of information out there that is just plain wrong. I find it difficult to know what's wrong from right, especially when it comes to UFOs! Biology and evolution I know, however.

SJ: Same here sir, sometimes it becomes hard to know whether the information is right or wrong.

JH: Yes it is, and I get stuff wrong in my books, but I am only human and UFOs are anything but!

SJ: Yes, by the way sir, what's your favorite topic on aliens related subject?

JH: At this time I am most interested in what the alien Grays actually are, what kind of life form they may be. I explore this in my book *Evolutionary Ufology* and more in my upcoming book *Little Gray Bastards*. [Now available.]

SJ: Amazing! Really it's really an amazing topic. Haha! I liked the name of your upcoming book *Little Gray Bastards*. I'm damn excited to read the book. By the way sir I would like to read your book *Evolutionary Ufology* so can please give me the link of it.

June 11, 12:48 a.m.

SJ: Sir, I want to get certified in Ufology. So, sir please tell me how to get certified in it?

JH: Get your graduate degrees. With a Master's degree you can be a research specialist for MUFON.

SJ: Okay sir.

June 14, 3:43 a.m.

SJ: Hello sir I want to discuss something very important with you on aliens. And I also want to discuss about teleporting. I have got a weird case and I think you will help me out.

JH: Sure! What's the case?

SJ: I came to know about a 5 years old kid who's talking about aliens or UFOs . . . his mom is so shocked that how her son knows about aliens because his mom never talked on such topics with him. When his mom asked him how do he know how aliens look, then he said that he have seen UFOs and aliens. Aliens come down and they have green legs and says in other places also have houses other than Earth and 84 UFOs have come from there. He also says he have touched their cold nose and they did not do anything to him. It's much more cold than his room AC inside the UFOs and he says he was there for 10 Earth days and they are combination of robots and humans. There were few seats inside the UFOs, which can be removed. There were 10 antennas. And one alien which was not ok, different than others. He also says he went when he was one. This is really strange to know that a 5 years old kid says all this things.

JH: Yes, it is strange. He could have a very vivid imagination, and maybe he has seen aliens and UFOs on television. If you can, have him make drawings of the aliens and the UFOs. Especially get him to draw and describe better the alien that was different and not okay. Once you have those drawings and descriptions we will have a better idea of what might be going on.

SJ: Okay sir! Sir, his mom says that she haven't told anything about aliens or UFOs to him and she has never talked on this with him.

JH: Interesting. Is it possible he saw science fiction on television?

SJ: No! His mom also said me that they were living in U.S. when her son was a year old.

JH: Definitely try to get the boy to draw the aliens and UFOs!

SJ: Okay sir.

JH: And then if you could send me the pictures that would be great!

SJ: Sure sir, as soon as I get the picture I'll send it to you.

JH: Thank you, Shreya. May I use this case in my next UFO book? I will give you full credit for the investigation, of course.

SJ: Thank you so very much. Umm, I have to ask his mom if she agree, then it's okay.

JH: Of course you should ask her.

SJ: Okay sir. She has no problem if you use this case in your next UFO book.

JH: Great! We'll write the chapter together, Shreya!

SJ: Here is the drawing. His mom has drawn this because her son isn't drawing it. His mom has drawn this according to what her son said.

JH: Great job, Shreya! Now see if you can get a UFO drawing.

SJ: Okay! The kid is very naughty. He isn't telling anything to his mom about UFO. His mom said me that she will try to ask him again after few days. And his mom also said me that her son is very sure that he has seen an UFO and alien and he said has been took to other place with aliens to the other planet which was very dark place. There was a seat for that kid and the aliens were driving the UFO. UFO was much more cold than his room AC. The aliens took him to the other planet. And he was there for 10 Earth days.

JH: Great work, Shreya! See if he will describe or draw the alien that "was not ok."

SJ: Thank you sir! No sir, he said aliens were good to him. They didn't hurt him.

JH: Oh, I thought you mentioned one alien that was different from the others.

SJ: Oh yes! Let me again ask his mom. Actually the kid is too moody. If he is in mood then only he answers to anybody's questions.

JH: Every case has its difficulties.

SJ: Yes. Good night sir.

June 16, 10:29 p.m.

SJ: David is asking to join us on our project. I don't know him properly. He is your friend so you says what should we do? I don't have any problem if he join us even I would like to work with him also.

JH: Oh, yes. David has been my friend for 25 years, and he and I are writing *Little Gray Bastards* together!

SJ: Oh! That's awesome! Should I make a group so that we all can talk together on this case?

JH: Sure. He and I are writing our next UFO book together, so your case would be in there, Shreya.

SJ: I'm feeling so happy that I'm working with you people. Yes and we will be friends.

JH: We feel the same way, Shreya. Anything new from the little boy and his aliens?

SJ: No sir, his mother told me that she will let me know about it after 2 days. Sir, the sketch of alien which I had sent you was made by his mother because the kid don't know how to draw it. So his mother sketched it. I just talked with his mother she told me about the structure of UFO, but she said she can't draw it, so I'm trying to draw it.

JH: Excellent! Looking forward to seeing that!

June 17, 9:22 p.m.

SJ: Hello sir!

JH: Hi Shreya! Good morning (?) to you and evening for me.

SJ: Yes! Good evening sir.

JH: What time of day is it for you?

SJ: Here it's now 10 o'clock. Thursday!

JH: Here it is 9:30 Wednesday night.

SJ: Oh! We are running fast.

JH: I have several chapters lined out for our next UFO book. No working title yet. Our first book, *Little Gray Bastards*, comes out sometime next year.

SJ: Sir, can you please send me some pictures of UFOs actually I had sent some photos of UFO but the kid is getting confused. So I want you to give some selected UFOs so that I can show that photos to that kid.

JH: Sure, I can do that. Hold on just a minute . . . Here's a graphic showing known UFO shapes.

SJ: Thank you sir. [Pause.] He has seen most of them. But this one especially.

JH: Really? And specifically this craft here?

A bell-shaped saucer identified by the young experiencer. *Acrylic on board, 11" x 14", by Jordan Hofer. Photograph by Jordan Hofer, 2016.*

SJ: Yes sir. As he mentioned he has seen 84 UFOs.
JH: I wish I could see just one!
SJ: Even I.

June 29, 10:24 a.m.

SJ: Sir, did you seriously dreamt aliens? What did you dreamt?
JH: Yes, I did. I was not joking. One time two Grays were looking at me only inches from my face. The first time, five Grays were standing at the foot of the bed looking down at me. The scary thing about this is that the "dreams" took place in the exact place in which I was actually sleeping.
SJ: Wow! So that happened with you in actual?
JH: I "woke up," scared as a baby screaming for its mama!
SJ: Hmm! So you fear aliens!
JH: Yeah, I'm scared of those little gray bastards!
SJ: Sir, I'm worried about my case. The boy is not answering anything.
JH: He is a difficult witness. And that is frustrating. But we do have some interesting information. We can do something with it.
SJ: Yes! But how?
JH: Sometimes a case only goes so far. Then you attempt to interpret what you have. You did a good job. Maybe the boy will talk more later on. Keep in touch with the mom.
SJ: Yes sir, I have told his mom to ask him again on this after a month.
JH: Great!

July 3, 9:05 a.m.

SJ: Hello sir, today is a big day for me. Today is the day when I join my team or I started working on the paranormal.
JH: Hurrah!

July 8, 8:12 a.m.

SJ: Hello sir! How are you?
JH: I am fine, thanks! How is your paranormal research going?
SJ: Oh! It's going okay, okay. Actually I'm busy these days so no give more attention towards it.
JH: What are you busy with?
SJ: As you know I got my job as an art and craft teacher in a school. So I'm trying to get settle properly there with works.
JH: Is that fun?
SJ: Yes sir, it's fun teaching children! I easily get attach with them. I'm really enjoying it. Even they are very happy with the new teacher. Hahaha . . . that's me.

JH: I did the same thing when I was your age. I taught science to little kids.

SJ: Wow! When you were young you were used to teach kids and I'm also doing the same thing. After that you started giving interest towards paranormal world.

JH: Yes! I didn't start in on UFOs until about 6 or 7 years ago. Before that I didn't believe in anything paranormal. I was a scientist and that was all!

SJ: Oh! That's interesting. But then how you started believing in all this things?

JH: My best friend of 35 years saw a black triangular UFO fly over his house.

SJ: Ohhh . . . What happened next?

JH: It rattled his windows with a loud noise, then floated away until it was out of sight.

SJ: Oh! Did he saw any alien?

JH: Yes, and so did his daughter. She called them "gnomes," and said that they played with her at night. She saw Grays. Her mom was crying. Yeah, and she talked about the bright lights outside her window.

SJ: She played with her?? Oh my God! Sir, let me tell you one thing. I was talking about a kid with you who saw UFOs and he went to many other planets. His mother had said me that her son was playing with them (aliens) and there were some toys for the kid to play.

JH: Toys, really? I've heard about that before. Did she say what kind of toys?

SJ: No, she didn't said what kind of toys were there. I'll ask all this to her after a month.

JH: Great!

SJ: As you know the kid is very naughty.

JH: Yes, he is! Too much!

July 17, 9:33 a.m.

SJ: Hello Jordan sir!

JH: Hello, Shreya.

SJ: Sir, yesterday I have a question. But sir, you promise me you will not laugh to my question! So yesterday I was thinking how do aliens breathe? If they come to Earth how do they breathe? Are they inhaling oxygen like we breathe or they are inhaling any other gases which are present on the Earth?

JH: That's a great question. Some people think the Grays don't breathe at all, that they are more like robots than a living species. Others think that the Grays are wearing spacesuits. My personal take is that they "breathe" through the skin and nostrils. I also think they get most of their oxygen from bacteria that live inside them. These bacteria are "fed" a high energy compound like hydrogen sulfide. Then the bacteria break down the hydrogen sulfide, giving energy to the alien.

SJ: Yes, sir totally agree with you! We all know that aliens have nostril so it is obvious that they might be inhaling any of the gases which are in their environment. I don't know how they actually breathe but you said through bacteria they used to take breathe. Yes, that can be. I think it's an interesting topic I should research on it! Also they do may have gills like fish!

July 19, 5:15 a.m.

SJ: Hello Jordan sir and David sir. Let's work together on this project.

DB: Hi Shreya. Jordan mentioned working on a UFO case with you. I'd like to hear about that case. You'll enjoy working with Jordan. He's extremely intelligent and one of the nicest people I know. And he has many good ideas.

SJ: Yes sir, I'm really enjoying working with him. Yes I agree with you that he's very intelligent and a good person. Okay, let me tell you the case. I came to know about a 5 years old kid who's talking about aliens or UFOs. His mom is so shocked that how her son knows about aliens because his mom never talked on such topics with him. When his mom asked him how do he know how aliens look then he said that he have seen UFOs and aliens. Aliens come down and they have green legs and says in other places also have houses on a planet other than Earth and 84 UFOs have come from there. He also says he have touched their cold nose and they did not do anything to him. It's much more cold than his room AC inside the UFOs. He says he was there for 10 Earth days and they are combination of robots and humans. There were few seats inside the UFOs which can be removed. There were 10 antennas and one alien which was not ok, different than others and he also says he went when he was one.

DB: Thanks for sharing this story with me. There are some very interesting details which ring true to me. I imagine Jordan also noticed these. One is that it's very cold inside the UFO—that's been reported by some witnesses, but is not well known in the larger culture. Another is that there are few seats. That one alien was different from the others and not "OK" is another such detail. Witnesses often report one alien who is different from the others, who is possibly in charge and seems hostile. The mix of aliens and robots has also been reported, but this seems like something that could be explained away as being fantasy if one were being skeptical. All in all, it's an intriguing report.

SJ: The picture of the alien is drawn by his mother because the kid couldn't draw.

JH: That is one weird picture!

DB: Shreya, I just wrote Jordan an email about some of the additional information you might try to collect from the mother. Jordan, can you pass that on to Shreya? I'm off to work soon so I can't do it now.

SJ: Okay David sir.

DB: Just some additional information you might try to get. You mentioned that there was a "different alien," one that was not "ok." What did that one look like? Also, some specifics about the sightings. When did the boy see the 84 UFOs?

JH: All at once, or over the years, or all when he was 5? Where did he see the 84 UFOs? From his bedroom window? While he was outside, in dreams? Where did he see the aliens? In his bedroom, in a dream . . .? Was he alone when he saw the aliens and the UFOs? Basically, see if you can get some specific locations and dates for the sightings. That would be very helpful. Investigating UFOs can be hard work!

The robotic alien as described to the young experiencer's mother. *Acrylic on board, 11" x 14", by Jordan Hofer, 2016 (from a sketch by the boy's mother). Photograph by Jordan Hofer, 2016.*

DB: It is hard work. The more specific the information gathered, the more seriously it will be taken by others besides us. If the little boy knows it was 84 events, he may remember many of them. Any details you can collect will be very helpful. Of course, we will protect his privacy. We don't need his name or exact location.

SJ: Okay sir, I'll ask these questions to his mother and I'll let you know about it.

July 20, 11:41 p.m.

SJ: He says the different alien has hands and legs which was different than the others. He is unable to explain how and about UFOs he says he saw most of them together while he was coming out of the UFO. There were also some floating rocks too.

DB: The floating rocks make me think of either an asteroid belt or the rocky debris in a ring around a planet, such as Saturn. Too bad he is not willing to draw these things.

SJ: Oh! Saturn. Jordan had sent me these two pictures to show that kid. The kid said that he has seen most of them but his specifying more to this one specific UFO.

JH: An asteroid belt, perhaps, yes. Possibly our Asteroid Belt. Might be base of operations.

SJ: Yes sir, it might be asteroid belt which is between Mars and Jupiter. As the kid said he was there for 10 Earth days. So while coming back to Earth he must have seen rocks floating around (asteroids).

JH: Shreya, did his mother notice that he was gone? It is possible that he was gone for ten Earth days his time, but only moments from the mother's perspective.

SJ: His mother said he has always been with her or in front of her eyes.

DB: During the abduction, he may have been on a different time track. That is often reported in abduction cases.

SJ: Oh!

DB: Time distortion is frequently reported in UFO abduction cases.

SJ: Okay.

JH: I was thinking the same thing.

July 22, 3:23 p.m.

JH: I think we can piece some of this together, and I will try. What we could use is a date when the boy was gone for ten Earth days (his time). Even though he was never out of his mother's sight, it is possible that she was "switched off" when the boy took his little adventure. It is also possible he was taken sometime during the night and then returned before morning (Earth time).

DB: Yes, that's plausible. A good question for the mom to ask the kid would be how long has this been going on, since what age? Also, how often does it happen, is it always at night or in the day time, where, what's he doing when it happens, etc.?

SJ: Okay! David sir and Jordan sir, I'll ask this to his mom. I remember his mom had said me one thing about it that he never talked on this before but suddenly one day her son said to his mom that she is looking different today! Something like alien! His mom was totally shocked because she had never talked on this with him and his mom then tried to contact me and the next day I told about this to Jordan sir.

DB: Got it. That is an interesting detail.
SJ: Yes.
DB: Thanks for sharing this with us, Shreya.
SJ: You are very welcome sir! David sir, I have asked some more few questions which you have told me to ask her. She said by tomorrow she will let me know about it.
DB: That's great, Shreya—thanks!

July 24th, 1:41 p.m.

SJ: Welcome! Jordan sir. The boy is very much naughty. He isn't answering to his mom's questions.
JH: Hmm . . .dead end?
SJ: Sorry! Sir, didn't get you.
JH: I meant that I think this investigation might be over.
SJ: No sir! I will try to get all the informations from that kid.

This concludes the frustrating case of the "naughty little boy" and his 84 UFOs. I do not know for certain if the boy was telling the truth, but many of his descriptions do have a ring of truth within the ufology narrative. Within this narrative I summarize the case below.

> A five-year-old boy remembers when he was only a year old and was abducted by cybernetic aliens, possibly early stage hybrids with technological enhancements. Referring to the boy's alien, the "hat" with its antenna may be some sort of EM (electromagnetic) or ESP amplifier. The angled piece covering the nose could be a hydrogen sulfide regulator, with the "mouth" as a part of the gas delivery system. The partial net-like covering over the face could be a permeable membrane that allows gases out but not in. The two hands with five digits on the right and six digits on the left are probably bifurcations of tentacles and thus have no analogous relation to the usual number of fingers on the human hand. The triangular shape of the body resembles a robe-like garment. The green "socks" are an equivalent of boots, and have been mentioned before in the literature on aliens. These strange aliens plucked the boy from his home onto their craft, which was very cold inside. He was abducted for ten Earth days, his time, and probably a single night at most from his mother's perspective. On his trip the boy saw 84 UFOs and on the way back to Earth he passed through our Solar System's Asteroid Belt. His reticence to answer more specific questions from his mother might have been implanted by the aliens or maybe the boy just doesn't want to remember anything further. He did mention another alien that was different from the cybernetic hybrids and "was not ok." I can only wonder what kind of interactions the boy might have had with this other alien during the ten days he was on board the craft. It is also remotely possible that the little boy invented everything and simply got bored with his imaginative game when his mom's questions multiplied. But how could he have concocted this tale if he had never been exposed to UFOs, aliens, and science fiction? Over to David:

As intriguing as this story is, the child's sudden unwillingness to speak about it places it in the category of hearsay at this time. I suggest that Shreya check back with the mother periodically to see if the child becomes more communicative. If he does, then the investigation should be resumed. The most interesting aspect of this case for me is that "It's much more cold than his room AC inside the UFOs." Someone making up a fictitious story about being taken aboard a UFO probably would not think of providing sensory details relating to the odors, sounds, or temperature inside the craft. There have been many cases in which witnesses report the interior of UFOs as being very cold. One such case is that of Alvin Guerra, who claims that in February of 1982, he was invited aboard a UFO staffed entirely by friendly, six-foot-tall, beautiful Nordic women. According to Guerra, "The interior of the ship . . . was extremely cold inside." (Reported by C. L. Turnage in the book *Sexual Encounters with Extraterrestrials*, Timeless Voyager Press, 2013, as quoted at www.thinkaboutitdocs.com/1982-january-march-ufo-alien-sightings/.) The little boy in Shreya's case also claims that he touched the aliens and they had cold noses. Again, this is a sensory detail you would not expect to hear from someone fabricating a lie or describing a dream or imaginary event. These details suggest there may be something real behind the little boy's story about having seen eighty-four UFOs and the strangely attired cybernetic alien.

Back to Jordan again: Though this case is closed with super glue, Shreya Joshi is still an emerging and recognized ufologist of the next generation. Indeed, it will take someone like Shreya to figure out the insoluble enigma of UFOs and aliens in the twenty-first century!

CHAPTER 2

CHAPTER 2

The Further Adventures of Earl Heriot

PART ONE

(by David)

In *Little Gray Bastards: The Incessant Alien Presence* (Hofer and Barker, Schiffer Publishing 2016) I discussed the case of Earl Heriot (a pseudonym). Heriot, who is now in his late sixties, claims to have had, over the course of his life, a number of mysterious experiences, some of which are paranormal in nature but do not appear to directly involve aliens, while others are alleged UFO sightings and what he feels are possibly encounters with aliens. Some of the events he reports are unequivocal memories of what Earl believes to be physical events occurring in the "real world," while others are puzzling mental images that have been present in his mind for many years, but that he is the first to admit may be merely products of his imagination or images that he has absorbed from the culture and internalized.

These unexplained events began about 1951, when he was three years old, and continued until the early 2000s, at which time they grew less frequent and eventually ceased—or so he thought. Heriot has always kept these stories very private, telling only close friends and family members about them. He agreed to allow me to write about his case on the condition that I use a pseudonym for him. In this and a later chapter, I provide an update on Earl's newly recovered memories related to three of the stories that I previously wrote about in *Little Gray Bastards*, discuss a few additional Earl Heriot stories that were not included in that first book, and tell of a strange new experience of Earl's that occurred about two years ago in 2015.

There are, at this writing, three different stories from *Little Gray Bastards* about which Heriot has had new memories surface since the book was completed. In all three cases, Earl was not consciously attempting to recover additional memories about the events; he thought he had already given me everything there was to say about these incidents. Earl might be able to learn more about these mysterious episodes in his life if he were willing to undergo hypnotic regression under the guidance of a trained therapist, but he's not interested in doing that.

How these new memories came about is that in each case he happened to be thinking about the mysterious event for no particular reason, mulling over the details of the experience that he consciously recalled, and suddenly realized that there was another "deeper" layer of memory just below the surface of consciousness of which he had always been aware but, for some reason, had not remembered when I interviewed him about the incident. In two of the cases, he was thinking about the layout of the incident's location, specifically the floor plan of the building where the incident occurred, when the new information rose into full consciousness. In all three cases, he was surprised by this "new information"—information which he says he had always known existed deep down inside—and was excited to tell me about it. And I, in turn, am excited to share it with the reader. Fortunately, Heriot seems to have shaken off the attack of paranoia that ended his work with me in *Little Gray Bastards*.

The Mantises (plural) in the Closets (plural)

One of the more bizarre stories that Earl Heriot shared with me for *Little Gray Bastards* was his vivid memory of there having been a secret "hidden closet" in the building where he attended junior high school (grades seven and eight) in 1961 and 1962. Heriot claims that he and the other children were periodically forced to enter that closet alone where they had a frightening encounter with a strange Mantid-type alien being. In Heriot's words this tall insectoid creature looked "a lot like a giant praying mantis." The hidden closet was located behind an inside wall in one of the classrooms that Earl visited every day. The children stayed in the tiny room for about ten minutes, during which time the alien performed an unknown procedure on them using a small hand-held electronic device that resembled an old-fashioned telephone receiver made out of shiny black Bakelite plastic. Earl and the other kids were terrified each time this unpleasant experience began and had to be literally dragged into the room by the teacher against their will, but they always came out in a calm state, quiet and subdued, as if the alien had used some form of mind control to sedate them and make them forget the experience. Earl says he never discussed these strange events with any of the adults in his life. He first related this tale to me in January of 2014. According to notes he had written years earlier, in 1991, the hidden closet was a small, oak-lined enclosure built into the wall of the classroom, and in addition to the fear induced by the experience, the students suffered considerable pain at the hands of the alien. In the notes, Earl documented a visual impression of the alien he had gotten from a dream: the creature was ten to fifteen feet tall, greenish-brown in color, and with a segmented body similar to that of a praying mantis. His notes indicate this species of Mantid aliens are known by their human subjects as "The Masters" because they exert total control over people everywhere, and that humans are bound in a secret cult-like allegiance to them. At the same institution, Earl witnessed a horrific scene after hours in his science classroom when the Mantid being, or one just like it, performed a medical operation on his science teacher, Mr.

Saltman (a pseudonym), who was stretched out naked on a counter where normally lab experiments were performed. In a mockery of a human doctor, the Mantid was garbed in a green surgical gown. That, in a nutshell, is the extent of what Earl consciously recalled about this series of events as of 2014.

Almost a year later, in December of 2014, Earl was thinking about the building where the Mantid experiences occurred and decided to draw a diagram of the building's layout. He made two pencil drawings that day: one of the general location of the hidden closet in the larger school building, and a "close-up" diagram of the closet, with the alien's position inside the small space, and his own position relative to the alien. He covered the rest of the sheet of paper with handwritten notes about these encounters. Because of some startling differences between this new document and Earl's earlier account of the Mantid events, I am providing the entire text of these December 2014, notes below.

Earl Heriot's further details on the Mantid in the hidden closet at elementary school [DB: in his manuscript, Earl changed "elementary" to "jr. high."]

The secret closet was in a large room at the far end of the school, possibly in the last room. As you entered the room from a long hallway, it was on the right side, through a door in a wood paneled wall. There was no window in the closet door.

The Mantid was very tall—7 or 8 feet, and had the appearance of a sculpted figure with sharp angles to its features, much like a Bishop chess piece. It was dark, possibly wearing a long robe, with oddly folding arms like the front limbs of a praying mantis insect. Its eyes were large, dark, and lacked visible pupils. The electronic device it held in its left hand was the general size and shape of a handset from an old-fashioned Bakelite rotary telephone. It may have had a black wire extending from its base. The Mantid may have had an articulated torso, like an insect.

Now, what's very odd about this new document is that Earl says that for the fifteen minutes or so during which he was working on it, he was picturing his elementary school, and not his junior high school. Was this simply a matter of his being temporarily confused about the location, or does it mean that similar encounters occurred during both his elementary and junior high school years? Note that his description of the alien is different for each location. Earl remembers the junior high school Mantid as being ten to fifteen feet tall and having greenish-brown skin, while the elementary school version of the Mantid was much shorter at seven or eight feet tall, was "dark" in hue, and possibly wore a robe. These sound like possibly different alien species.

By chance, Earl may have recovered a long-suppressed memory of unsuspected alien encounters during his elementary school years simply because he happened to be thinking about the physical layout of the location, and apparently new information surfaced. If, in fact, that is actually what happened, it suggests suppressed memories of interactions with aliens are not very deeply buried in the witness' subconscious, and may be retrieved through meditation alone.

I asked Earl if perhaps he had been merely confused while making his notes and drawings in late 2014, and if it is possible that the Mantid encounters only happened while he was in junior high school.

"I don't think I was confused at all. I remember these weird things happening both in junior high and elementary school. But for some reason, I only thought about the events at the junior high when I first told you this story. Drawing that floor plan, I was clearly picturing the elementary school, and oddly enough, the location of the secret closet within the building was very similar at both schools. It was in a classroom at the end of the building, on the right side when you came into the room from the hallway. The two schools were fairly similar in their layout. I think there were secret closets at both schools. I just didn't remember that until I drew the floor plan."

Ideally, I would like to see floor plans for both schools, but in this age of heightened security, that kind of sensitive information is not readily available. If I ever get a chance to visit either school, I want to see if I can find any signs that there is now or once had been a small closet built into the inside wall of the last classroom at the end of the building. It's been more than half a century since Earl was in elementary or junior high school, and public buildings can undergo numerous changes over that many years. If there ever was a secret closet at either school, the building could have been remodeled and the room walled up decades ago. Determining just how real Earl's memories about these two schools are would not be a simple task. But clearly, something very unusual must have happened to create such bizarre memories in a child. In contrast, Earl has no memories of anything mysterious having happened at his high school.

Return to Boron

In 1965, when Earl Heriot was in high school, he accompanied his best friend, Pete Marcusi and Pete's father on a weekend trip to Boron, California, to visit Pete's grandfather who lived alone in the desert in a ranch-style house just outside the town.

Boron, located north of Edwards Air Force Base, on the western edge of the Mojave Desert, is famous for its extensive deposits of the mineral borax and features the world's largest open pit borax mine. A mysterious and terrifying experience that Earl had on the first night he was there may bear some relationship to the presence of borax in the area. More about that later.

To this day, Earl doesn't have a full recollection of exactly what transpired after he and Pete retired to their sleeping bags in the living room of the house that night. All he knows for sure is that it was easily the most frightening night of his life.

They drifted off to sleep peacefully, and the next thing either of them knew they were standing outside of the house in the cold darkness just before dawn, raw with emotion, frightened beyond their ability to express. The sun was about to rise in the East, breaking through the clouds lining the horizon. In Earl's own words, "It was like the light was making the evil darkness scatter and hide." Earl did not know why he felt such an incredible fear. All he knew was that some unspeakably horrible thing had transpired within the black sea of night that surrounded and engulfed the house during the hours after midnight. Earl says that two words formed in his mind as he struggled to understand what had happened: "They came."

Until very recently, Earl didn't know who "they" might be. When he asked himself this question, there was no answer anywhere in his conscious memory. He always suspected "they" might be alien visitors, but that was just a theory, because he believed he remembered nothing beyond the fact of their unwelcome arrival at the house after dark. Oddly, he did have a notion that whoever they were, they came from out of the east, which would be in the direction of Barstow, and beyond it, the Mojave Desert.

That summarizes what Earl had originally told me about his experiences in Boron. My initial investigation of his case had come to a sudden end when Earl grew tired of my constant probing of his memories and wanted nothing more to do with the subject of UFOs and alien beings. However, he softened this stance over the months that followed, and once his paranoia about the subject of aliens had subsided, he began to think again about the Boron incident, particularly about the layout of the grandfather's house. One day he phoned me to report that a new memory had surfaced about the Boron event:

> I was thinking about the floor plan of that house. It was fifty years ago, but I remember it pretty well. The house faced east, with the living room at the front, the garage on the right or south side and kind of to the back, and—I think—a kitchen with a side entrance on the left or north side. There were two bedrooms in the back, on the west side of the house where Pete's dad and granddad slept. Me and Pete bunked down in the living room. And then I got to thinking about how there was this long hallway in the middle of the house that ran from north to south for the entire length of the house, with the bedrooms off of it on the one side, so that the hall was between the living room and the bedrooms. And suddenly, when I thought of that hallway, a new memory came to me from out of the blue. Or rather, a memory returned, because I've always known this thing, from the start. It came in the form of a strong mental image. I'm in the dark hallway, in the middle of the night, and the hallway is full of people! What are they doing there? It's crazy! So many people that we're packed in there like sardines. I can see the heads of some of them, even though it's very dark and what I see is faint. These people are taller than I am—I have to look up at them—and they have blue skin! Their heads are large and bald, and there are so many of them that it's more like they're animals than human beings. What I mean is that they're like a swarm of tadpoles in a pond or something. They give me the impression of being a herd, rather than individuals. And I don't understand who they are or what they're doing there or why I'm in that hallway. I just know that I feel sick about it, that it's a terrible thing. That's where the memory ends.

Earl swears that the memory was there, buried in his subconscious, all along, but that it never was accessible to him when I interviewed him about this experience. He was quite surprised to have recovered this shocking memory a year after having told me about the Boron incident and feels that it goes a long ways towards confirming what he intuitively knew from the start: that this mysterious event in the desert somehow involved aliens.

As mentioned earlier, the area where Pete's grandfather lived was rich in borax—so much so that Earl and Pete came across countless towering piles of pink borax crystals during the course of their weekend, while every few minutes a dump truck filled with the material would race past them on one of the many dirt roads crisscrossing the desert near the house. This constant industrial traffic suggests the house was in the immediate vicinity of the mine site. At no time has Heriot theorized a connection between the abundance of the rare mineral in the area and the possible presence of aliens. And yet, just such a connection has been documented in the UFO literature. In her book *UFO Headquarters: Investigations on Current Extraterrestrial Activity* (1999), Susan Wright quotes an anonymous informant using the alias "Jarod-2" who claims that the government has had a secret partnership with aliens dating back to an alleged UFO crash near Kingman, Arizona, in 1953, and that the aliens are "mainly trading with the US government for boron, a relatively scarce element." Jarod-2's supposed authority in this matter comes from his claim that he worked as a consultant for thirty years on a secret government project designing UFO flight simulators.

Another documented correlation between alien visitors and the mineral boron dating to around the time of Earl Heriot's experience in the desert near Boron is found in Mort Young's book *UFO: Top Secret* (1967). As part of the investigation into a wave of UFO sightings in Michigan in the spring of 1966 (the famous "Swamp Gas" case), samples from the site of a reported UFO landing near Hillsdale College were scientifically examined. According to Young, "An extensive series of soil and water tests later revealed the presence of the element boron in the earth and on the surface of the lagoon. This finding seemed significant—but of what? The arboretum soil was Miami loam, which does not contain boron. Stranger still, the element was found in its pure form. Boron does not occur in this state naturally; it must be manufactured." Although he doesn't go so far as to speculate on specifically how aliens are using pure boron, Young points out that humans use it in atomic reactors, in the manufacture of steel alloys, and in missile fuel (pages 54–55).

Another document connecting boron to aliens is a 1995 article in *The Groom Lake Desert Rat*, an online newsletter at www.ufomind.com/area51/desertrat/1995/dr24/#boron. The article's informant is the same anonymous witness cited by Susan Wright: Jarod-2. According to the article, "'All I know is they [aliens] sure take a lot of boron,' Jarod remarked cryptically at one of his talks before a small UFO group. When pressed for possible reasons, Jarod then remarked that, among other things, boron is useful for preserving human bodies—a suggestion that caused some consternation among the abductees in the audience. When pressed, Jarod admitted that this was merely speculation on his part and that he didn't have any information that the aliens were using boron to ship bodies." The article goes on to say that most of the world's boron "is extracted from a big hole in the ground at—you guessed it—Boron, California, which happens to be adjacent to the most secret part of Edwards Air Force Base" and that other major boron mines in the US are also located near military bases and in areas known to be "UFO hotbeds." While it's tempting to speculate that Edwards Air Force Base is located there because the mineral deposits in the area are an attraction for alien visitors, the base was established in the 1930s, a decade before UFOs became an issue for the Air Force.

Months after telling me about the newly recovered hallway memory, Heriot had a sudden insight into something that had puzzled him since high school. About 1965, he made a small painting depicting a group of nude humanoid figures, all with blue skin, who are in a desert-like environment with a tall rock spire in the foreground.

The beings are facing away from the viewer and appear to be hailing the rising sun that is positioned just above the horizon. Or, depending on how you look at it, they are bidding farewell to the setting sun. There is dark sky above and long, shadowy clouds clustered along the horizon, one of which crosses the solar disk. Heriot says he always thought of the blue people as being aliens, which was odd because he didn't give much thought to the subject of UFOs in high school, and as far as he recalls, this is the only artwork he did during high school that had aliens as its subject. He never knew where the idea for the painting came from; it always seemed

Earl Heriot's 1996 painting *Attack of the Soft Blue People,* which he believes depicts alien humanoids he encountered in Boron, California, in 1965. *Photograph by Earl Heriot, 2016.*

quite mysterious to him. Although he gave the painting to a friend in high school, it continued to be important to him for unknown reasons, and in 1996, he made a copy of it from memory, which I've seen. One day, while we were discussing his memory of blue aliens crowding the hallway at Pete's grandfather's house, Earl suddenly thought of the small painting and wondered if there might be a connection between this mysterious work of art and his bizarre experience at Boron. While he doesn't remember if the painting was done before or after the trip to Boron, he is confident that it was done around the same time. Oddly, he never associated the trip with the painting until very recently, and likely wouldn't have made the connection had we not been talking about the Boron incident in detail again.

There is documentation in the UFO literature for the presence of blue-skinned aliens in the Mojave Desert area. Ron Felber's excellent book *Searchers: A True Story* (1995) tells the gripping tale of a couple who were held captive overnight in the Mojave wilderness by aliens with "grayish-blue bodies" and "laser-like, red eyes" (page 98). Notably, this case also highlights the alien pursuit of minerals. During a long night of captivity trapped inside their camper, the terrified couple observe an alien-controlled machine they call a "probe" that locates and recovers minerals from deep within the earth in an apparent mobile mining operation that involves loud grinding noises and intense vibrations (page 102).

Another Glimpse of the Occupants

The third, and most recent of Earl Heriot's strange stories in *Little Gray Bastards* for which new details have emerged since the book's publication is the one titled "The Long Beach Blimp UFO." This was a series of multiple UFO sightings that Earl experienced over the period of about a month in early 1982 (roughly mid-February through mid-March). The sightings fall into two distinct phases.

Phase One, which lasted about a week, began when Earl was driving home from work on the San Diego Freeway around 6:30 p.m. one evening shortly after sunset. As he entered Long Beach, California, and was approaching the Long Beach Municipal Airport, he spotted a dark aerial object approximately one mile away, on his left, north of the freeway. When he got to within a half-mile of it, the object crossed over the freeway and was then on his right side. Once he reached the airport, the object was about a quarter mile away, hovering approximately 500 feet above Long Beach General Hospital. The hospital, located at the intersection of E. Willow Street and Redondo Avenue, closed in November 1983, according to an article in the *Los Angeles Times* dated March 2, 1986. This site is on the eastern edge of the Signal Hill district, but is on relatively level land and not at or near the top of the hill. The significance of this will later be made clear. Heriot says the object was football-shaped, approximately 150 feet long and fifty feet tall, with a gondola-like cabin on the bottom that measured about fifty feet long and ten feet high. The surface of the craft was a dull, non-reflective black color and it had one or two rows of dim red lights running horizontally along the side. Yellow light came from inside the cabin. Through the cabin windows, he could see wall panels with electronic equipment and possibly maps on them and humanoid occupants who were about seven feet tall, appeared to be male, and had large bald heads, oval eyes, and gray skin. They wore tight fitting silver-gray-colored uniforms with horizontal pleating on the chest. This initial sighting lasted a minute or two. Later the same week, he saw what he thinks was the same craft two or three times more. These sightings really didn't register in his consciousness and he quickly forgot about them. He always saw the Phase One UFO near the hospital as he was driving home on the freeway.

Phase One was followed by an interim period of about two weeks during which he did not see the UFO on his drive home from work. Early in this period, on a Saturday night, he happened to be listening to the *Open Mind* radio talk show hosted by Bill Jenkins when Jenkins and his guest, noted ufologist Dr. J. Allen Hynek, discussed reports Jenkins had received that week of a UFO seen by multiple witnesses over the Long Beach Airport. The description of the object being reported closely matched what Earl had seen that same week, and this information had the effect of unblocking the suppressed memories of his own sightings. He quickly realized that he, too, had been seeing this unidentified flying object. During the two weeks that followed the radio program, he looked for the UFO on his drive home each weekday, but didn't see it. On Saturday night, a week after the program aired, while they were driving home from a movie, Earl and his wife, Jane, suddenly decided to go hunting for the UFO. They spent a half-hour driving up and down the freeway and side streets around the airport looking for it, but they didn't see anything unusual in the skies over Long Beach.

Phase Two, which occurred during the fourth week of the one-month period over which the entire series of sightings lasted, began when Earl saw a decidedly different-looking UFO as he was driving home on the San Diego Freeway one evening and was entering Long Beach near the airport between 6:30 and 6:45 p.m. This object was the same size and shape as the Phase One UFO, and like it, had a flat black body, but the red lights along the side were not visible, and instead it had a large "sign board" on the side that functioned like a TV screen and displayed constantly changing brightly-colored geometric patterns along with symbols that Earl called "hieroglyphics." The cabin affixed to the bottom of this craft was unlit and dark. During the following days of Phase Two, he saw the object at various points along the freeway from the "South Bay Curve" on into Long Beach, a distance of about twelve miles. It seemed to be playing a game of "cat and mouse" with him, hovering in a stationary position as he approached it and then suddenly disappearing and instantaneously reappearing a considerable distance away, as if it had dematerialized from one place and then rematerialized in another. One evening at the end of the Phase Two sightings, Earl got off the freeway before he reached his normal exit and chased the UFO through the streets of Long Beach for several blocks, but he was unable to catch up with it, although he did manage to get within a couple hundred yards of it at one point.

That, briefly, is Earl's original story about the Long Beach Blimp UFO sightings. Given the long and detailed report that Earl had written shortly after the events happened, I assumed no more information about the sightings would be forthcoming from Earl, but I was wrong. In February 2016, I received the following email from him in which he describes two additional memories about the Long Beach Blimp UFO that had recently surfaced in his conscious mind while he was idly mulling over the events of 1982.

> I just realized there is a weird detail about the Long Beach Blimp UFO that has always been part of my memory of the incident but that I never thought to tell you about for some reason. It has to do with a "visualization" I had shortly after the sightings, a mental image of the aliens occupying this tall, transparent, cylindrical shaft-like structure that extended down from out of the sky above the UFO, passed through the body of the craft, and then extended farther down through the air below the UFO and into the hospital building as the UFO hovered directly over the hospital. It was like a huge glass tube that connected the UFO with the hospital, but in another dimension—not in our normal everyday physical world. The shaft had many floors in it that were subdivided into rooms—all of it transparent—and aliens could be seen all through the inside of the tube, on all the floors. They were taller than the Grays I saw through the UFO's cabin windows with my normal physical vision. They had white skin and gray uniforms, and I got the impression they were doing some important medical work, both on board the UFO itself and in the hospital below. That they were hanging in mid-air over the hospital for a long time . . . for many hours, possibly even days . . . doing this important work, and I should just forget about them and leave them to it. I didn't put this visualization into my report on the sightings because it was too weird and the basic sightings were incredible enough without adding a bizarre paranormal experience in which I saw how the UFO was connected to the hospital by a big glass tube-like thing.

As if this recent revelation wasn't startling enough, Earl described another newly recovered memory in that same email.

> Also, I keep asking myself if Jane and I didn't go up to the top of a hill in Long Beach, maybe it was Signal Hill, one night during the second phase of the sightings to what was supposedly a "hospital" building, although I don't think it really was a hospital, where we stayed for about an hour. I have the impression that we immediately decided this was a very bad idea—that we were at considerable risk there—and that we left as soon as possible. I don't remember anything specific about what happened to us inside the hospital . . . just walking up to it on a bush-lined sidewalk in the dark, on top of a hill. This might have been on the Saturday night that we went searching for the UFO. This memory—if that's what it is—only seems half real to me. I vaguely recall us doing that, but at the same time it also feels like a bad dream or some crazy fantasy. As with the "glass tube" memory, this "hospital visit" memory was present in my mind when I wrote my narrative, but I suppressed it as being just too damned weird.

As I previously noted, the former Long Beach General Hospital was situated on flat land on the edge of Signal Hill and not at a higher elevation on the hill proper, so it could not have been the supposed "hospital" building that Earl believes he and Jane may have visited one night during the Long Beach Blimp UFO sightings. The exact nature of the hilltop building they allegedly visited remains a mystery.

CHAPTER 3

CHAPTER 3
The Rendlesham Code Reconsidered

(by Jordan)

> I've gone on record saying Rendlesham might be the turning point in history that leads to the explanation of the UFO phenomenon.
>
> —Nick Pope
> UK Ministry of Defense UFO Project
> 1991–1994

The Rendlesham Forest incident is such a high-profile case that I do not treat its narrative in this chapter. My attention is focused on the claims of Jim Penniston, USAF (Retired), who encountered a triangular craft in the forest near two United States Air Force bases in Britain after midnight on December 26, 1980 (Pope, 2014). Staff Sergeant Penniston touched the craft's surface, which he described as smooth. He noticed several strange glyphs on the craft and recorded them in a notebook. When he placed his fingers on the glyphs he found they were rough like sandpaper. Suddenly, his mind was filled with binary, a "neural download" of zeros and ones from the craft.

After the encounter, Penniston filled sixteen pages of his notebook with the binary code, the zeros and ones flowing from his pencil until he felt he had written all of them out of his brain. Much later, Penniston gave the code to "Professional Binary Code Expert" Joe Luciano (for more information visit Luciano's website at www.binarydecoder.info/main.php). Amazingly, the binary supposedly coded for a very strange message:

EXPLORATION OF HUMANITY 666 8100
52.0942532N 13.131269W
CONTINUOUS FOR PLANETARY ADVAN???
FOURTH COODINATE CONTINUOT UQS CbPR BEFORE
16.763177N 89.117768W
34.800272N 111.843567W
29.977836N 31.131649E
14.701505S 75.167043W
36.256845N 117.100632E
37.110195N 25.372281E
EYES OF YOUR EYES
ORIGIN 52.0942532N 13.131269W
ORIGIN YEAR 8100

Penniston believes that this is a message not from aliens but from time-traveling humans from the future. The longitude and latitude coordinates "read like a New Age holiday wish list" (Pope, 2014: 245): Caracol, Belize; Sedona, Arizona; Great Pyramid in Giza, Egypt; Nazca Lines in Peru; Tai Shan Qu, China; Portal at Temple of Apollo in Naxos, Greece.

"Is all this just wishful thinking?" Pope suggests. "Or is the message more subtle?"

I tend to believe that the message is, if not "more subtle," probably far more complex with layers of code hidden in a multitude of codes within codes—many ways to read the code and translate it into meaningful messages.

Luciano's translation is very odd. "HUMANITY 666 8100" is the first red flag. Do humans in the future, "ORIGIN YEAR 8100," still read and interpret the Book of Revelation from the Bible? Because the "666" is just silly. The first and last coordinates given are for the mythical lost island of Hy Brasil. Apparently this is where our future time-traveling descendants come from. Why is the word "ADVANCE" decoded as "ADVAN???"? I'm no master code breaker, but I bet I can guess the

ALIEN GLYPHS

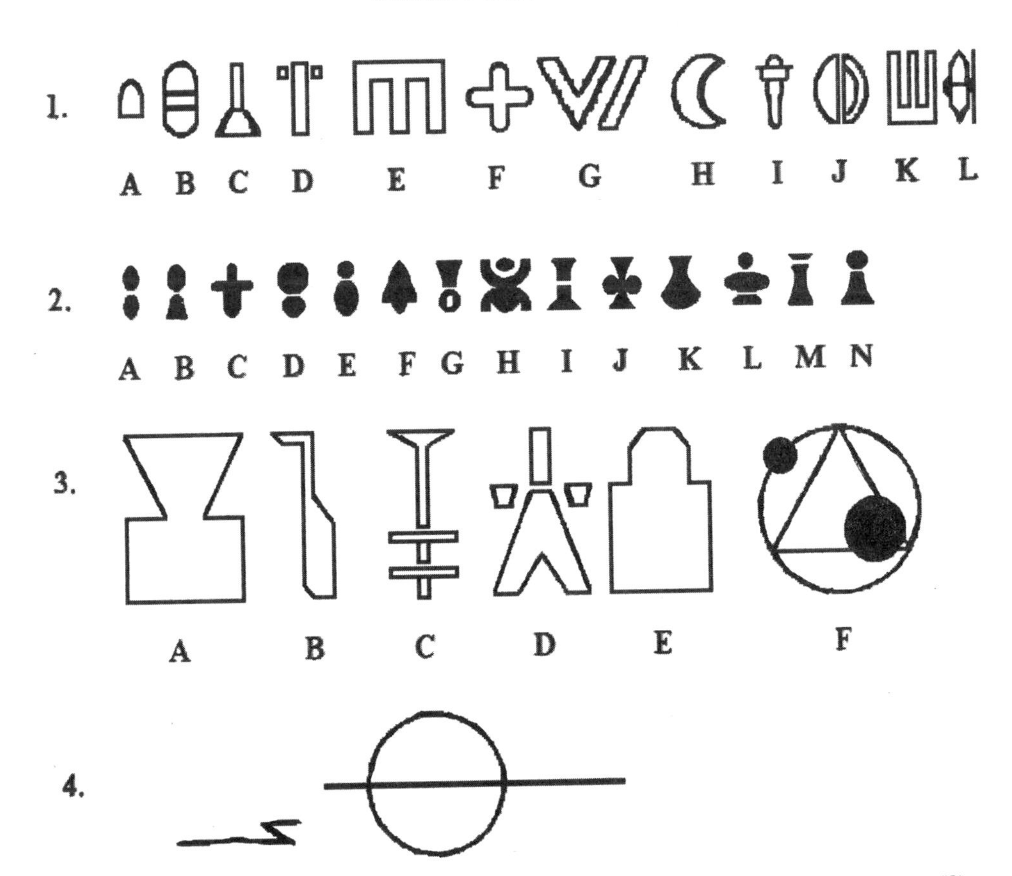

Alien glyphs from 1) the Kecksburg craft, 2) the Roswell I-beam, 3) the Rendlesham Forest craft, and 4) the Ted Owens "SI Disk." *Illustration by Jordan Hofer, 2016.*

last three letters where those question marks are. Why could not Luciano? The same argument holds for "COODINATE" and "CONTINUOT," obviously "COORDINATE" and "CONTINUOUS." The only other explanation is that future humanity makes spelling errors. "UQS" and "CbPR" are meaningless to me. And "BEFORE" what? That sounds like trouble. The next six coordinates comprise the "New Age Holiday wish list." And then there is the oddly poetic, if not clichéd, "EYES OF YOUR EYES." "You are the apple of my eye"; do they still have that expression in the year 8100? Do they still have apples? The message ends with "ORIGIN YEAR 8100," the reason Penniston believes the craft was constructed and operated by time-traveling humans. I have tried to keep an open mind about Luciano's translation, but I think it's wackadoodle.

"Is there a more complex message hidden deeper within the obvious one? I have no answers here. Maybe other experts will come up with an alternative translation" (Ibid).

Later in the chapter I offer an "alternative translation" of Penniston's binary code. But first the glyphs on the craft demand attention for a translation of their own. Alien symbols from three craft and one artifact are compared and used as referents to one another (see figure above): the Kecksburg craft (1), the Roswell I-beam (2), and the Rendlesham Forest craft (3), as well as Ted Owens' SI (Space Intelligences) Disk (4).

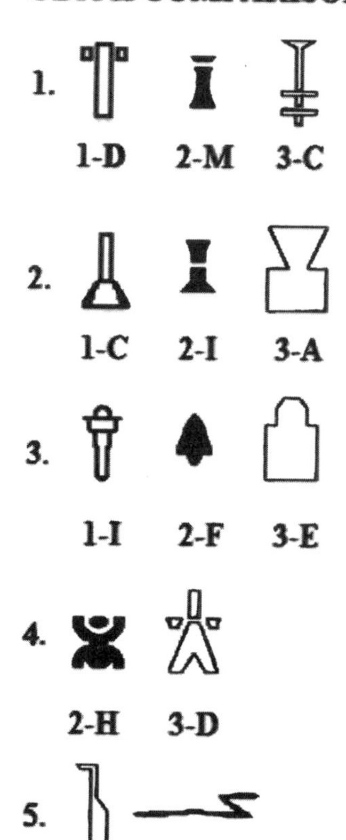

Comparison of specific glyphs from the four sources. *Illustration by Jordan Hofer, 2016.*

In the above figure, comparison of symbols 1-D, 2-M, and 3-C suggest, within the context of the Rendlesham code, the translation of "communication." Symbols 1-C, 2-I, and 3-A are deciphered as "base of operation," in this case, "Earth." 1-I, 2-F, and 3-E all look similar to some sort of "spacecraft." Symbols 2-H and 3-D appear anthropomorphic and are interpreted as "humanity." 3-B and 4-A both denote an "advance" from home star systems.

Therefore, once reconstructed, the Rendlesham glyphs read, "Earth Advance Communication [with] Humanity Spacecraft [from] Zeta 2 Reticuli," which is precisely what the craft did—communicate—when Penniston touched the glyphs and received his neural download of binary code.

The symbols in the figure that follows come from the Rendlesham craft and the SI Disk, respectfully, and denote the location of the alien home planet. Since the only known extraterrestrial star map comes from the Betty and Barney Hill abduction, I must assume that the home planet's origin is in the Zeta Reticuli binary star system. 1-A is the larger of the two suns and is, therefore,

GLYPHS OF STAR SYSTEM ORIGIN

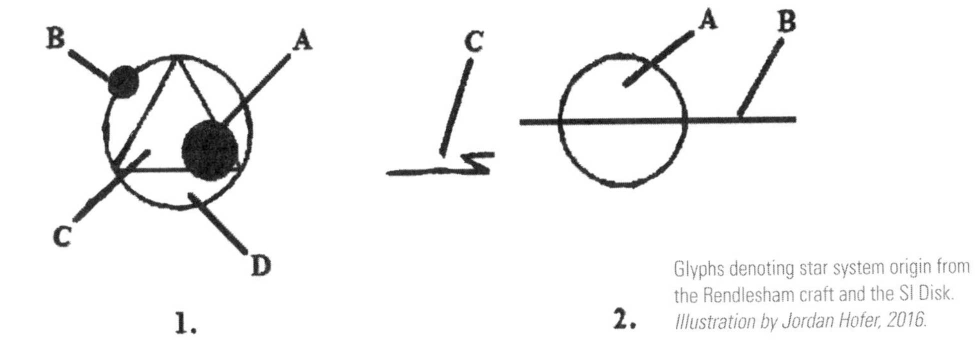

Glyphs denoting star system origin from the Rendlesham craft and the SI Disk. *Illustration by Jordan Hofer, 2016.*

Zeta 1 Reticuli; 1-B is Zeta 2 Reticuli and is located on the symbol for the home planet, tellingly revealing that the aliens' home star is Zeta 2 Reticuli. 1-C is the same shape as the equilateral triangular craft from the Rendlesham incident and probably represents the craft. 1-D is the home planet, identity unknown. The SI Disk offers an interesting comparison to the Rendlesham symbols. 2-A is Zeta 2 Reticuli, and 2-B is the home planet's elliptical orbit around the alien sun. 2-C is the symbol for "advance," in this case, advance of SI power from the aliens to humans for whom the disk functions as a communication device.

I have no way of confirming my above speculations, but I believe I have interpreted the codes correctly and certainly to the best of my ability. I have seen others present their interpretations of the Rendlesham symbols and found them lacking. Surely I can do no worse than any other. The comparisons and conclusions reveal a self-contained logic, which suggests all four sources for the symbols are part of the same language.

But the symbols are not the only codes in the Rendlesham mystery. The binary code that was downloaded into Penniston's brain is a powerful set of information comprised of 4,360 digits. As I transcribed the zeros and ones from Nick Pope's book into my word processor I began to feel lightheaded and then nauseous. By the time I finished I nearly vomited.

01000110010011101010101010101001001010100010010000100001101001111
01001111010001000100100101001110010000010101010001000101010000110
10011110100111001010100010010010100111001010101010011110101010100010
10101010100010101001110010000110110001010101000001010010010000100
10001010100011001001111010100100100010101011000010100000100110001
00111101010010010000010101010001001001010011110100111001001111010
01110100100001010101010011010100000101001110010010010101010001011
00100110110011011001101100111000001100010011000000110000001101010
01100100011000000111001001101000011001000110101001100110011001001
00111000110001001100110011000100110011001100010011001000110110001
110010101011101000011010011110100111001010100010010010010100111001010

1010100111101010101010100110101000110010011110101001001010000100
11000100000101001110010001010101010001000001010100100101100101000
0010100010001010110010000010100111000011100100010010000101000101 0
0110010011011000110111001101100011001100110001001101110011011101 00
11100011100000111001001100010011000100110111001101110011011000111 0
0001010111001100110011010000111000001100000011000000110010001101 11
0110010010011100011000100110001001100010011100000110100001100110 11
010100110110001101110101011100110010001110010011100100110111001101
1100111000001100110011011001001110001100110011000100110001001100 11
0011000100110110001101000011100101000101110010001101010011011000 11
1000001101000011010101001110001100010011001001100010011010000110 11
1001100000011000100110101001100000011010101010011001101110011010 10
0110001001101100110111001100000110100001100110101011100110011001 10
1100000110111001100010011000000110000001101100011001100110010010 00
1010011001100110111001100010011000100110000001100010011100100110 10
1010011100011001000110101001100110011011100110010001100100011100 00
0110001010001010100010101011001010001010101001101001111010001100 1
0110010100111010101010101001001000101001100101000010101010011010 0
1111010100100100100101000111010010010100110001101010011001000110 0
0001110010011010000110010001101010011001100110010010011100011000 10
0110011001100010011001100110001001100100011011001110010101011101 00
1111010100100100100101000111010010010100111001011001010001010100 0
001010100101011100000110001001100000011000 0

At this point I didn’t know what I was going to do with the zeros and ones from Penniston’s brain. But an episode of the science fiction series *Orphan Black* gave me an idea. Two of the characters used binary to break a code that held genetic information. Perhaps the binary coded for alien proteins or else important proteins involved in human reproduction. The hell if I know. But searching for genetic codes within the binary just makes sense. I had to translate the zeros and ones into the four nucleotides in DNA: adenine, thymine, cytosine, and guanine (A, T, C and G). Four nucleotides generate twenty-four possible permutations of genetic code:

1) A = 00, T = 01, C = 10, G = 11
2) A = 00, T = 01, C = 11, G = 10
3) A = 00, T = 10, C = 01, G = 11
4) A = 00, T = 10, C = 11, G = 01
5) A = 00, T = 11, C = 01, G = 10
6) A = 00, T = 11, C = 10, G = 01
7) A = 01, T = 00, C = 10, G = 11
8) A = 01, T = 00, C = 11, G = 10
9) A = 01, T = 10, C = 00, G = 11
10) A = 01, T = 10, C = 11, G = 00
11) A = 01, T = 11, C = 00, G = 10
12) A = 01, T = 11, C = 10, G = 00
13) A = 10, T = 00, C = 01, G = 11

14) A = 10, T = 00, C = 11, G = 01
15) A = 10, T = 01, C = 11, G = 00
16) A = 10, T = 01, C = 00, G = 11
17) A = 10, T = 11, C = 01, G = 00
18) A = 10, T = 11, C = 00, G = 01
19) A = 11, T = 00, C = 01, G = 10
20) A = 11, T = 00, C = 10, G = 01
21) A = 11, T = 01, C = 00, G = 10
22) A = 11, T = 01, C = 10, G = 00
23) A = 11, T = 10, C = 00, G = 01
24) A = 11, T = 10, C = 01, G = 00

Each permutation translates the zeros and ones in Penniston's binary code into a very long list of As, Ts, Cs, and Gs. Two numbers code for each nucleotide; e.g. 11 is A, 10 is T, 01 is C, and 00 is G in permutation twenty-four. The original set of zeros and ones is broken into 2,180 numerical pairs:

01 00 01 10 01 00 11 10 10 10 10 10 10 10 10 01 00 10 10 10 00 10 01 00 00 10
00 01 10 10 01 11 10 10 01 11 10 10 00 10 00 10 01 00 10 10 01 11 00 10 00 00
10 10 10 10 00 10 00 10 10 10 00 01 10 10 01 11 10 10 01 11 00 10 10 10 00 10
01 00 10 10 01 11 00 10 10 10 10 10 01 11 10 10 10 10 00 10 10 10 10 10 10 00
10 10 10 01 11 00 10 00 01 10 11 00 01 01 01 01 00 00 01 01 00 10 01 00 00 10
01 00 01 01 01 00 01 10 01 00 11 11 01 01 00 10 01 00 01 01 01 01 10 00 01 01
00 00 01 00 11 00 01 00 11 11 01 01 00 10 01 00 00 01 01 01 01 00 01 00 10 01
01 00 11 11 01 00 11 10 01 00 11 11 01 00 01 11 01 00 10 00 01 01 01 01 01 00
11 01 01 00 00 01 01 00 11 10 01 00 10 01 01 01 01 00 01 01 10 01 00 11 01 10
01 10 11 00 11 01 10 01 11 00 00 01 10 00 10 01 10 00 00 01 10 00 00 01 10 10
10 01 10 01 00 01 10 00 00 01 11 00 10 01 10 10 00 01 10 01 00 01 10 10 10 01
10 01 10 01 10 01 00 10 01 11 00 01 10 00 10 01 10 01 10 01 10 00 10 01 10 01
10 01 10 00 10 01 10 01 00 01 10 11 00 01 11 00 10 10 10 11 10 10 00 01 10 10
01 11 10 10 01 11 00 10 10 10 00 10 01 00 10 01 01 00 11 10 01 01 01 01 01 00
11 11 01 01 01 01 01 01 00 11 01 01 00 01 10 01 00 11 11 01 01 00 10 01 01 00
00 01 00 11 00 01 00 00 01 01 00 11 10 01 00 01 01 01 01 01 00 01 00 00 01 01
01 00 10 01 01 10 01 01 00 00 01 01 00 01 00 01 01 01 10 01 00 00 01 01 00 11
10 00 01 11 00 10 00 10 01 00 00 10 10 00 10 10 01 10 01 00 11 01 10 00 11 01
11 00 11 01 10 00 11 00 11 00 11 00 01 00 11 01 11 00 11 01 11 01 00 11 10 00
11 10 00 00 11 10 01 00 11 00 01 00 11 00 01 00 11 01 11 00 11 01 11 00 11 01
10 00 11 10 00 01 01 01 11 00 11 00 11 00 11 01 00 00 11 10 00 00 11 00 00 00
11 00 00 00 11 00 10 00 11 01 11 01 10 01 00 10 01 11 00 01 10 00 10 01 10 00
10 01 10 00 10 01 11 00 00 01 10 10 00 01 10 01 10 11 01 01 00 11 01 10 00 11
01 11 01 01 01 11 00 11 00 10 00 11 10 01 00 11 10 01 00 11 01 11 00 11 01 11
00 11 10 00 00 11 00 11 00 11 01 10 01 00 11 10 00 11 00 11 00 11 00 01 00 11
00 01 00 11 00 11 00 11 00 01 00 11 01 10 00 11 01 00 00 11 10 01 01 00 01 01
11 00 10 00 11 01 01 00 11 01 10 00 11 10 00 00 11 01 00 00 11 01 01 01 00 11
10 00 11 00 01 00 11 00 10 01 10 00 10 01 10 10 00 01 10 11 10 01 10 00 00 01
10 00 10 01 10 10 10 01 10 00 00 01 10 10 10 10 10 01 10 01 10 11 10 01 10 10

10 01 10 00 10 01 10 11 00 11 01 11 00 11 00 00 01 10 10 00 01 10 01 10 10 10
11 10 01 10 01 10 01 10 11 00 00 01 10 11 10 01 10 00 10 01 10 00 00 01 10 00
00 01 10 11 00 01 10 01 10 01 10 01 00 10 00 10 10 01 10 01 10 01 10 11 10 01
10 00 10 01 10 00 10 01 10 00 00 01 10 00 10 01 11 00 10 01 10 10 10 10 01 11
00 01 10 01 00 01 10 10 10 01 10 01 10 01 10 11 10 01 10 01 00 01 10 01 00 01
11 00 00 01 10 00 10 10 00 10 10 10 00 10 10 10 11 00 10 10 00 10 10 10 10 01
10 10 01 11 10 10 00 11 00 10 11 00 10 10 01 11 01 01 01 01 01 01 00 10 01 00
01 01 00 11 00 10 10 00 01 01 01 01 00 11 01 00 11 11 01 01 00 10 01 00 10 01
01 00 01 11 01 00 10 01 01 00 11 00 01 10 10 10 01 10 01 00 01 10 00 00 11 10
01 00 11 01 00 00 11 00 10 00 11 01 01 00 11 00 11 00 11 00 10 01 00 11 10 00
11 00 01 00 11 00 11 00 11 00 01 00 11 00 11 00 11 00 01 00 11 00 10 00 11 01
10 01 11 00 10 10 10 11 10 10 01 11 10 10 10 01 00 10 01 00 10 10 00 11 10 10
01 00 10 10 01 11 00 10 11 00 10 10 00 10 10 10 00 00 10 10 10 01 01 01 11 00
00 01 10 00 10 01 10 00 00 01 10 00 0

Each numerical pair codes for a specific nucleotide and, when the transcription is complete, a short series of nucleotides (three binary pairs long), called codons, can be translated into amino acids and strung together into short proteins. The above code contains 1,453 codons. Not every nucleotide sequence is translated, however. Only strings of code with start and stop codons are considered valid in this endeavor (AUG for methionine and start codon; UAA, UAG, and UGA for stop codons). Further, only proteins twenty amino acids and longer are considered valid molecules, referencing that the shortest known protein on Earth (this is a bias that could lead to error) is only twenty amino acids long, known as TRP-Cage and found in the saliva of Gila monsters (www.science20.com/princerain/blog/smallest_protein). Following these rules for translation, nearly every permutation produces proteins of twenty or more amino acids.

Take, for example, permutation three of the above code. Permutation three is coded A = 00, T = 10, C = 01, G = 11. The first three pairs of binary code are 01, 00, and 01 which transcribe as the codon CAC which translates to amino acid histidine (abbreviations His and H); CAU also codes for histidine. Note that the nucleic acid codon has uracil (U) in place of thymine (T). There are twenty common amino acids, most with more than one nucleic acid code, and three amino acids that code for "stop": alanine (abbreviations Ala and A; codes GCU, GCC, GCA, and GCG), arginine (Arg and R; CGU, CGC, CGA, CGG, AGA, and AGG), asparagine (Asn, N; AAU, AAC), aspartic acid or aspartate (Asp, D; GAU, GAC), cysteine (Cys, C; UGU, UGC), glutamic acid (Glu, E; GAA, GAG), glutamine (Gln, Q; CAA, CAG), glycine (Gly, G; GGU, GGC, GGA, GGG), histidine (His, H; CAU, CAC), isoleucine (Ile, I; AUU, AUC, AUA), leucine (Leu, L; UUA, UUG, CUU, CUC, CUA, CUG), lysine (Lys, K; AAA, AAG), methionine and "start" codon (Met, M; AUG), phenylalanine (Phe, F; UUU, UUC), proline (Pro, P; CCU, CCC, CCA, CCG), serine (Ser, S; UCU, UCC, UCA, UCG, AGU, AGC), threonine (Thr, T; ACU, ACC, ACA, ACG), tryptophan (Trp, W; UGG), tyrosine (Tyr, Y; UAC, UAU), valine (Val, V; GUU, GUC, GUA, GUG) and the "stop" codon (UAA, UAG, UGA).

The results of translation from nucleic acid sequence to amino acid sequence for the twenty-four possible permutations are listed below:

PERMUTATION 1:

NO SEQUENCE

PERMUTATION 2:

MYLSILINTYLSNFIVTYPI

MGVCVGECTHNGCGRVCNA

MYGCVRVCINEEGGQEGWSDSRSFLVLQDFTTLVVI

MNVLTDLHTVRHTHIHTYRLSGRSGSRTVGQQEGRVSMSE

PERMUTATION 3:

MIRPPSPDYPSRPSSTHPDFLTKSAR

PERMUTATION 4:

MYVCKLVSDVRGHILTDARTNTRDYTQTDTQTYELEAYGRTNERDYRHVC

MFVSFCVCLYVTHKLVFLCVKSVCK

PERMUTATION 5:

MHLSMNISHDIYIHIYIDQCHLDPSMNQSHDT

PERMUTATION 6:

MEGSTGRRCAMRKHASKPASKYASEPARDVARAHARTRASTLQPSVPTTDRGIGGMELDGR

MYAYIDVCDHQSIDRCMYASGYI

MHESEVHGCINEWDHRYARQLASTPASPRARPHAMYKPAPSRAKLARKQASARHRALARTQARTPRSEPARSRASKHHPPYHPAVHTTVGGRGYQGMIGRRSDG

PERMUTATION 7:

MHKNIKSTINININASLIPPHD

MTEKVSACMSECLCDMLCVCMCV

MLYVTHLRTYSPTYPHTHPLT

PERMUTATION 8:

MGDCRTDGVMDCWGVGRTDWVMDWGTGWGVGL

PERMUTATION 9:

MYLSMRAPFIFVYMPCIYPSMHIYSYICIYLSI

PERMUTATION 10:

MDVLIDLYIVRCIYVYMYRSTFLDYLRL

MLAGKAASVCIDLWMYLWIFISIYVSHAD

MDGSIYSVIYLCMYGCTYFTIDLYIYR

MASRRASARSCERASARACIRFLL

PERMUTATION 11:

MDGATDRRGAGRMDRATDRGMGRGAGSQSKPTTDLQT

MARRIKNDNSAKLLNDEHTNSGRQPDYLANSLDCSLSHSLTR

PERMUTATION 12:

MTHTRTHAQTDALRPSMPAASQKVKKVRQLSKE

MRRPPQYVCTCVSMYSRRSVSEYVCTSKCV

PERMUTATION 13:

MRTTSYIHTFNHSLHAPVYD

MSVHTIRHSYKHSKTQTNIQCVFNHKDTQFRHTFIQSHTITHRHTYIHTYKTSLKHTDTHSFIINKVIKQRM

PERMUTATION 14:

NO SEQUENCE

PERMUTATION 15:

MFVCLDDLVGACLDGFVIACMPV

MYVETSNQSKDDCIFAFFACMP

MFLWFDYWLCLWLQSRWKNMLAR

PERMUTATION 16:

MLHTYMPNYSSYVFAHDRSCVRPRVSTRARSRARTSDSCTFVRPSVSTLAYITRYLHKYLKI

MHKMLSKYIDIYLPTTNKATK

PERMUTATION 17:

NO SEQUENCE

PERMUTATION 18:

NO SEQUENCE

PERMUTATION 19:

MSIPFLLAPSLTCSPSFYLTCFPSA

MRSLGRALHRARVRACARSWEVGRHGCCLAP

MRAVERSCGRSGARAGVRYIFGRGSARFERAFVVRSRAVARERACVRACGASLGRASARSFVVGGMVGRQV

PERMUTATION 20:

MGLVVRGCVRSWGWLYVRSLGCR

MLVRGGVGSAVGVGVGTDLVPPRS

PERMUTATION 21:

MSYCVRAYLAVIHAYLHAVSHTYSHTCQHTLTHTLMHPVLT HSCSHPFQHSRAWLSACVGAWGCEWVRDIHLAVGVCDLCLPDCVSRCVSACVPAYVGYCLGV

PERMUTATION 22:

NO CODE

PERMUTATION 23:

MHARRQTVIGTHSHPPTHSEC

MHADRHPHSASHTHAHTQSAMADSGSHPARASRTVCSYVRLFVRFCVCLSVQTPFVFMCVPYVCPSVRVCSCVYVCLSV

PERMUTATION 24:

MMDRASDRQTDAQRDGWREGVTLVSCLSVRLALPTDTQSDRSTDRWRDSMRERARERLTDPPVTD

MSESVLLSGCLSGFFSIFLSRQRLALYLSRLSVWLASSLVFSLSVCLAVSLFSSLSLYLARRLLFV

Note that every protein begins with M, the symbol for methionine and the amino acid that signals the beginning of translation into amino acids from the nucleic acid RNA code. From the lengthy analysis of the DNA permutations, five contain no codes (permutations 1, 14, 17, 18, and 22). Permutation 1 (A = 00, T = 01, C = 10, G = 11) does have one string of code but it is only nineteen amino acids long, just shy of the 20+ rule. Permutation 14 (A = 10, T = 00, C = 11, G = 01) has three chains, the longest of which is composed of only thirteen amino acids. Permutation 17 (A = 10, T = 11, C = 01, G = 00) contains no codes at all; there is not even a single methionine, start or otherwise. These odds seem strange out of 1,453 codons, perhaps seemingly improbable. But any given codon has a 1/64 chance of being methionine. And out of 1,453 codons we can expect approximately only twenty-three methionine, so the conspicuous absence of any code whatsoever isn't really improbable at all! The other permutations with no codes are just as unremarkable and only five out of twenty-four contain no admissible code. The remaining nineteen permutations comprise, all told, forty-one proteins. Are all the proteins identifiable or do only some of the proteins actually exist? I am no biochemist and I have had a most frustrating time attempting to identify these chains of amino acids. Furthermore, as with any scientific endeavor, confounding variables conspire to compound error and doubt.

The first problem with the above analysis is that I transcribed the binary code from Pope's book only once and had no one to check my work (also, Penniston's notebook pages 14, 15, and 16 are written in very light graphite and difficult to read); any number of digits may be incorrectly transcribed, altering the code, and there are 4,360 digits (or chances) potentially leading to error. After breaking up the binary code into numerical pairs, a single zero remains at the end of the code. Is it possible that I read the code incorrectly and the lone zero is at the beginning of the code instead of the end? This would create a frameshift mutation and the entire code would produce completely different amino acid sequences.

I am also no computer programmer, so every permutation took approximately four hours to arrive at the amino acid sequences; the twenty-four permutations used up a hundred hours of research time. That's far more time than I spent on my genetics homework back in college!

Another more devastating discovery throws the entire work above into total rejection altogether. Luciano claims that the pages of Penniston's notebook are printed out of sequence in Pope's appendix (pages 263–270), as follows: 4, 1, 2, 3, 5, 6, 7, 8, 10, 9, 11, 12, 13, 14, 15, 16. Luciano and Pope share the same sequence for ten notebook pages: 5, 6, 7, 8, 11, 12, 13, 14, 15, 16. This shared buffer is no defense against a frameshift mutation or the misreading of a single nucleotide among

1,453 codons; nor does the translated code match the following transcription of binary according to Luciano:

0100010101011000010100000100110001001111010100100100000101010100
1001001010011110100111001001111010001110100100001010101010011010
0000101001110010010010101010001011001001101100110110011011001110
0011000100110000001100000011010100110010001100000011100100110100
1100100011010100110011001100100100111000110001001100110011000100
0011001100010011001000110110001110010101011101000011010011110100
1001010100010010010010100111001010101011011110101010101010011010
0001100100111101010010010100000100110001000001010011100100010101
1010001000001010100100101100101000001010001000101011001000001010
1110000111001000100100001000011001001110101010101010100100101010
0100100001000011010011110100111101000100100100101001001101000101
1000011010011110100111001010100010010010100111001010101010011110
1010001010101010100010101001110010000110110001010101000001010010
1000010010001010100011001001111010100100100010100110010011011000
1011100110110001100110011000100110111001101110100111000111000001
0010011000100110001001101110011011100110110001110000101011100110
1001101000011100000110000001100000011001000110111011001001001110
1100010011000100110001001110000011010000110011011010100110110001
1110101011100110010001110010011100100110111001101110011100000110
1001101100100111000110011001100010011000100110011001100010011011
0110100001110010100010100110001001101000011011100110000000110001
1010100110000000110101010100110011011100110101001100010011011001
1100110000011010000110011010101110011001100110110001100100011010
0110110001110000011010000110101010111100011000100110001001101110
1000100110000000110000001101100011001100110010010001010011001100
1110011000100110001001100000011000100111001001101010100111000110
0001101010011001100110111001100100011001000111000000110001010001
1000101010110010100010101010011010011110100011001011001010011110
1010101010010010001010011001010000101010100110100111101010010010
1001010001110100100101001110001101010011001000110000011100100110
0001100100011010100110011001100100100111000110001001100110011000
0110011001100010011001000110110011100101010111010011110101001001
1001010001110100100101001110010110010100010010011001010100001110
0011100011001100000010110000

This time, I felt no nausea as I transcribed the binary sequence, perhaps because I was typing the correct sequence? But I do not know if it really is correct. When I transcribed the "Pope version" I got 4,360 digits, 2,180 nucleotides, and 1,453 codons. In the "Luciano version" I ended up with 4,365 digits, 2,182 nucleotides, and 1,454 codons. Not a large difference between the two, but enough to skew the data entirely. Perhaps another four hours of research time is warranted in translating at least one permutation of the Luciano binary sequence. I again broke the code into pairs of zeros and ones, as before.

I translated the first permutation sequence (A = 00, T = 01, C = 10, G = 11) of the Luciano code and present it below.

LUCIANO PERMUTATION 1:
MTLTSSPPLPTNILPATTYSTHPA

The permutations from the Pope and the Luciano sources don't match. In the Pope version, Permutation 1 produces no proteins. Permutation 1 of the Luciano version has one protein, twenty-four amino acids long. What in hell it codes for I have no idea. If I had more time I would go through one hundred more hours of research on the Luciano version of the binary code.

Hopefully, someone with more knowledge than I have in biochemistry and computing will crack the genetic code(s) I am still convinced resides in the binary message from the Rendlesham Forest. Unfortunately, all the Reader can take away from this, in my opinion, is a sensible translation of the glyphs on the Rendlesham craft. Was it worth over a hundred hours of arguable madness?

Reconsiderations Reconsidered by David

I have long suspected that, given the complexity of reported alien activity, there very well may be multiple meanings embedded in the binary code received by Jim Penniston. It seems quite feasible to me that 1) Joe Luciano's translation of the code is accurate, and 2) that an additional message in the form of scientific information is built into the code, such as the genetic information that Jordan postulates.

I disagree with Jordan's dismissal of Luciano's translation. For most of my life, I have been a professional research analyst, and for the past twenty-five years I've specialized in data analysis. Although I know almost nothing about binary code or biochemistry, my instincts as an analyst tell me that Luciano, who follows a careful, conservative, and fully documented methodology in translating the binary code, is probably right. The message he derives from the data is so close to being completely intelligible that the small amount of "nonsense" in the form of apparently meaningless junk characters is almost certainly due to errors in the data. The presence of these errors does not discredit the translation. Almost all data sets contain errors, especially if it is "secondhand" data and not the original raw data.

Jordan questions why highly advanced humanoids from the future would make typos in the message, such as "COODINATE CONTINUOT UQS CbPR BEFORE." But that assumes the aliens are the source of the errors. Given that Penniston waited a day before he wrote down the binary from memory, it's far more likely that he is the source of the errors, and that he garbled a message that was correct when he downloaded it from the craft. As a series of cryptic ones and zeros, it's amazing that he could recall any of the code, let alone most of it. Luciano's text is very likely an accurate translation of Penniston's flawed transcription. For example, the nonsense phrase "CONTINUOT UQS" becomes the meaningful word "CONTINUOUS" if the "T," a space, and the "Q" are deleted as being merely noise in the signal.

I also disagree with Jordan's take on the line "EYES OF YOUR EYES." I don't sense that this is intended to have a poetic value, comparable to "You're the apple of my eye." It's far more likely the phrase is akin to the human term "EYES ONLY" that is sometimes placed on classified documents, signifying they are intended for only a specific set of readers, and are not to be copied or photographed. Another possibility is that the line refers to the huge, oval-shaped eyes of the Grays and the smaller and rounder eyes of humans, suggesting that their bodies evolved from our bodies, as they are our future descendants.

Jordan's arduous attempt to decode the binary as a genetic code is fascinating, although so complex that I'm afraid I don't fully understand it. I think he may be onto something real, although it needs further work. A data analyst who understands biochemistry could use computer programming to speed up and simplify what, for Jordan, was obviously a grueling task of manually extracting scientific information from Penniston's cryptic series of ones and zeros.

CHAPTER 4

CHAPTER 4
The Further Adventures of Earl Heriot
PART TWO

(by David)

In *Little Gray Bastards*, I explored Earl Heriot's lifelong history of UFO sightings and encounters with apparent alien entities. As exhaustive as that discussion was, by its end I had arrived at no solid conclusions as to just how real Earl's experiences were, nor exactly what they meant, if anything. But there was more to Earl's story, and in this book I continue that exploration, offering up new stories, expanding on old ones, chasing down the few hard facts that can be established, and searching for whatever solid meaning I can extract from his ever deepening story. In the process, I've learned more about Earl as a person and a witness, and have gleaned further intriguing details about his often highly bizarre experiences, but I have not solved their mystery by a long shot. I still do not know anything definite about the unidentified aerial objects he has observed: where they come from, their true nature, nor why they are here. I still know almost nothing about the weird beings he has received visits from on many occasions. I don't know if they are extraterrestrials, or "locals" who—unrecognized by us—are native to this planet. I don't know if they are physical biological creatures, induced false memories, or non-material paranormal entities. I don't even know if they are friend or foe—whether their intentions towards humans are good, evil, or indifferent. And, remarkably, I can't even prove there is a connection between the UFOs Earl sees and the so-called "aliens" that visit him.

What I *can* say with certainty is that he's a credible witness, and I have no reason to doubt the truthfulness of what he tells me. Researching his case has been both fascinating and frustrating at the same time. I've learned a great deal, but there is so much more that I do not understand. I'm still no closer to solving the UFO mystery. Lacking any discernible over-arching message or pattern, Heriot's lifetime of random weird happenings appear to have no purpose beyond the perverse satisfaction that aliens seem to derive from toying with human minds and emotions.

Nonetheless, I am convinced it's a story worth telling, if only in the hope that someday keener minds than mine may be able to unravel what it all means. Still, this presents as another dwindling probability of solving the experiences.

Sleeping in the Car

During the writing of *Little Gray Bastards*, Earl Heriot mentioned in passing that he had some strange experiences that possibly may be related to UFOs and aliens on two different trips that he and his family took in the mid- to late-1950s. I didn't have time to research those incidents and interview Earl about them at the time. When I finally got around to asking Earl about these incidents, he told me that unfortunately he currently remembers very little about them—only that on a summer vacation during which they traveled by car across the US from their home in California to various points east, the family spent the night in their parked car on two occasions when a campsite or hotel room was not available, and he suspects that both times they were "visited" and possibly abducted by aliens. Then, on a second vacation trip a couple years later, he saw what he thought at the time were "angels" in a small church where his family attended a service. For some reason, he sensed there might be a connection between the earlier alien encounters and the later angelic apparition.

If that's all there was to this set of weird stories, they would still be worth mentioning in that they add weight to his other stories of suspected alien encounters during childhood. However, luckily, there is more—much more—to tell. For in 1987, when Heriot still retained far more detailed memories about these incidents, he wrote a full account of them in the form of a supposedly "fictional" horror story titled "Little Church in the Pines."

> "I didn't have the guts to write these up as non-fiction reports of UFO and paranormal phenomena," says Earl, "but I wanted to document the events while I still remembered them well, so I put it all into this short story. The first two-thirds of the story is set in the 1950s and is basically everything I remembered about these really strange trips I took as a kid. This part is straight autobiography. It's factual. The rest of the story is set thirty years later in the 1980s, and in it the grown hero of the story takes his own daughter on a similar trip in which they retrace the path he and his family took on their 1955 trip. That part is pure fiction, completely made up.

Earl Heriot still has the unpublished manuscript of "Little Church in the Pines" and he loaned it to me for evaluation. He had not reread the story since he wrote it in 1987. I was stunned by what I read, for it contained a great deal more detail than I'd hoped to get about these incidents at this late date. His descriptions of the alien encounters, and the fantastic vision of "angels" that followed, are so vivid, I quote the entire first two-thirds of the manuscript below. I do not include the final third of the story because it is fictitious by design, and doesn't tell us much about Earl's real life involvement with aliens, other than revealing some wishful thinking on his part when, as author, he has the hero's daughter, who had been kidnapped by aliens (that's fictional and didn't really happen), returned by the benevolent angels.

One thing that puzzled me about the story is the age of the unnamed hero, called "the middle boy," who is ten years old in the summer of 1955. He represents Earl, and Earl was seven in 1955, not ten. Earl explains that he probably changed his and his brothers' ages so it wouldn't appear to be an autobiographical story, but conceivably he may have instead changed the dates. Given this, the real life date of the first trip is either 1955, when Earl was seven, or 1958, when he was ten, and the angelic apparition was either in 1957, when he was nine, or in 1960, when he was twelve. Further research among Earl's family papers may eventually resolve this question. The detail about ages and dates is the only fiction in the following account.

Excerpts from "Little Church in the Pines"

August 1955

They were driving through the Mojave Desert, a family of five in a four-door Chevy sedan. The land was hot and dry and flat. At every small town, they stopped for Cokes or malts in a futile attempt to cope with the suffocating heat of the desert.

The father enjoyed traveling. He sang popular old songs he had learned in the service as he drove along the endless straight highway. Or, he told humorous stories to his wife. She, in turn, spent most of the day studying the road maps they had picked up for free at gas stations, monitoring their slow progress along the network of red lines crisscrossing the country. When she wasn't busy playing navigator, she did what she could to keep the kids happy: doled out small toys, suggested simple games, passed out snacks.

The kids were basically miserable. Trapped in the car on what seemed to them a pointless voyage through a landscape of relentless desolation and inhospitality, they fell into a kind of half-waking, half-sleeping stupor. They daydreamed, fought, dozed, complained.

The oldest boy, a teenager, felt himself somehow aloof to the whole experience. An unwilling participant. He couldn't wait for the vacation to end and reminded his parents of this at least hourly.

The youngest boy, a seven-year-old, was probably the most content of the three kids. His suffering was largely physical; he was too hot, too thirsty, his legs were getting stiff from sitting all day in the cramped confines of the backseat. He was the easiest to sooth, the mother found. A malt and a quick stroll through a parking lot would keep him happy for another three or four hours on the road.

The middle boy—the ten-year-old—well . . . the mother wasn't sure how he was handling it all. He seemed—as usual—to be lost in a daze. Lost in a dream world of his own. He enjoyed the malts, played the guessing games ("the next license plate we see will be a Utah . . . the next car we pass will be a Packard . . ."), but it seemed as if his heart wasn't really in it. He wasn't completely with them. His mind wandered off—to where, she couldn't guess. She imagined his soul just drifting off, out of the car, out over the desert, dissipating into the wide open spaces.

She worried about him, probably unnecessarily. He'll come around, she reassured herself, folding up a map and laying it on the scorching hot metal of the dash. He'll snap out of it. It's just a phase he's going through . . . .

They passed Navajo huts with colorful spreads of blankets and pottery and silver jewelry out on display in front of them, for sale to tourists. Sometimes they stopped—against the husband's strong protests—and bought a few trinkets to show the people back home.

They drove through whole dry forests of cacti and eucalypti. And once, they stopped for a half a day in a petrified forest, a forest of broken and jumbled stone logs.

They visited some caverns, spent the day on a guided tour into the depths of the dank caves. And when they came out, the bright sunlight hurt their eyes and gave them all headaches. That evening, they saw the tremendous cloud of bats—millions of the creatures—rising like smoke from the yawning mouth of the cave. It was quite a sight, the black mass of them fanning out against the fading red hues of the sunset.

And one afternoon, as they drove through the desert, the middle boy thought he saw a gigantic insect—a butterfly with a two-foot wingspread—fluttering between the barrel cacti along the side of the highway. He asked his mom about it and she said to "ask your dad." So he did, and the father stopped singing. "I don't believe they get that big, son. At least not in this part of the world." And that was that.

But that night, as they sat in their tent in the nearly empty campgrounds, the middle boy again saw the huge insect. Actually, all he saw was its shadow as it passed between the glowing wicks of the Coleman lantern and the gauze screen covering the tent doorway. He let out a tiny scream—more surprise than fright—and his mom just laughed. "Why honey," she said, "it just looks big because . . . well because . . ." She couldn't explain it, and she let the father take over. "Because of the angles involved. The bug—the mosquito—looks so big because it's near the lantern, and its shadow is being projected onto the tent door. But it's just a normal-sized bug, no bigger than the ones we have at home."

It sounded like a good explanation, a rational one, and he accepted it.

They traveled for days through the desert, stopping each night in one of the camp spots Mom had circled on one of her maps. And then, one night, they couldn't find the campsite, or it was closed—the boy didn't remember which it was—and they had to make-do by parking along the roadside in a big dusty turn-out that trucks used, and sleeping in their car.

None of them liked it. It was uncomfortable, trying to get a good night's rest sitting in the car, and the fact that they had spent all day in there just made it that much worse. "Where's your pioneering spirit?" the father asked, trying to cheer them up, but nobody answered him. They didn't have any pioneering spirit; what they wanted was a clean, air-conditioned motel room, and if they couldn't have that, then they wanted their tent and sleeping bags and air mattresses.

But they managed to get to sleep anyway.

And later, in the wee hours of the morning, when everything outside the car—the still and quiet desert—was shrouded in darkness, they were visited.

It was the first visitation of the trip.

The boy—the ten-year-old—never knew if the other members of his family were aware of the visit. He never discussed it with any of them, didn't mention it to his brothers or Mom and Dad.

In his memory, it didn't seem like much. Some lights coming toward the Chevy. Truck lights, he figured, aroused from his dreams. He was afraid the truck driver wouldn't see their car parked along the edge of the turn-out, that he would hit them. That they would all be killed as they slept, or worse, horribly injured. The lights came very close, bore down on them mercilessly. He couldn't understand why no one else was awake, why none of them sensed the lights. Were they all in some hypnotic state, some trance that wouldn't allow them to wake up, to escape?

In the morning, as they drove on, he tried to recall what had happened next. The lights came close—flooded the interior of the Chevy. Then they stopped, and some shapes became visible—dark figures in front of the light—and they approached the car. They gathered all around and peered into the windows at the sleeping family. Maybe a dozen of them. And he saw their faces—their horrible faces. Not the faces of men.

He considered asking his father about it, but didn't. There was probably some perfectly normal explanation for it. Like the insect shadows on the tent door. And he didn't want to look stupid in front of his brothers. So he tried to forget about it.

But what had they wanted?

He felt he probably knew, if he could only remember the words they had spoken to him. Foreign words that he shouldn't have understood, but did. Words that passed through the glass like radio waves, like TV transmissions, straight into his young and receptive brain.

A week later, half a continent away, they entered a cool green valley thick with forest. The sound of running streams accompanied them as they pressed eastward. Now the heat of the desert was just a strange memory.

The boy forgot about the night spent in the truck turn-out. Forgot about those alien faces pressed against the car windows. He no longer remembered the strange sounds of their speech, nor the import of their message.

One day they had car trouble, and spent all afternoon in the waiting room at a dealership while mechanics worked on the Chevy. That same night, they had some bad luck at a motel. The place had looked okay at first glance, and they'd taken a room. But once inside, they discovered that the room was infested with some kind of small insects—fleas most likely. The boy had been lying on a freshly made bed, staring idly at the wall when—to his horror—he noticed that the "polka dots" on the wall paper were moving, were alive. They checked out and found a campsite in a park fifty miles up the road, where they spent the night instead.

The next few days of their trip were uneventful. In a way, the boy kind of missed the desert. In spite of the terrible heat, the starkness and desolation of the Mojave, it was more fun, more interesting than the bland, banal greenness of the woods. This part of the trip seemed all blurred together in his memory. Aside from the car breaking down and the flea-infested motel, there wasn't all that much worth remembering about it.

Until the second visitation.

Once again, they had been unable to find room at a campground, and had resorted to sleeping in the car while parked in a tree-shaded city park in some small town. It had seemed like such a nice park in the late afternoon with all the millions of leaves blocking out the blue summer skies and the expanses of green lawn just fringed with a touch of yellow deadness. They all slept better that night than they had at the truck turn-out, more deeply, more easily.

And then, after midnight, they came.

He could see them through the frosted glass of the rear window. Backlit, a large number of them, approaching the car.

And once again, the strange, foreign sounding speech, calling to him, imploring him. They wanted him to come out, to leave the car, leave his family behind, forever, and go with them. He almost did as they asked, almost gave in to their persuasive voices.

They came closer—some of them actually touching the doors and windows with their thin elongated fingers—and the sweet song of their calling changed to harshness and threats. Then he knew it was wise not to join them but to stay in the car.

As before, he was the only one to wake up during the visitation; the other family members seemed drugged, dead. His whimpers and cries had no effect on any of them. He was alone in his fear. In his panic.

And then, as quickly as they had come, the creatures were gone. He was grateful to be left behind, with his family, in the security of the locked car, and he cried himself back to sleep while the cold light of the moon fell across his face through the rolled up window.

The next morning he told his mother he had had a bad dream. She said it was due to sleeping in the car. "You'll sleep better tonight," she assured him. "We'll be at your aunt's by dinnertime."

July 1957

Two summers later, they returned east. Nothing happened along the way—nothing that stood out in the boy's memory—but there was something unusual that happened on the evening before their return trip to the West Coast.

For some reason unknown to him—his parents weren't the least bit religious—they attended services at a quaint little church situated deep in the woods, a few miles from his aunt's house. What he remembered best about the church later, when he thought about that strange evening, was the way it seemed to be so full of light. A radiant golden light that gave off warmth. Maybe it was all the wood—the paneling and the ornate carvings above the altar.

He felt at home there. Peaceful. As if he had finally arrived at the one safe place in the universe, the one place where the strength of God's goodness would protect him from all harm. He sat close to his mother, her hand holding his, and he thought to himself: this is really the best part of the trip . . . I am happy here . . . I wish we could stay here and never leave, stay in this warm, glowing little church. Over to one side, under a statue of the Virgin Mary, a cluster of candles flickered in red glass cups. He thought he smelled the scent of fresh roses, and wondered where it came from. He didn't see any flowers on the altar, or anywhere else.

The organist was playing and a choir was singing—the words were in Latin. He didn't know what the lyrics meant literally, but still, he seemed to understand the message of the song, and was moved by it.

And then, the unusual event—something so bizarre that he knew immediately that he would never forget it.

He saw them around the altar—against the deep orange luster of the wood carvings—angels—genuine angels. Living angelic creatures. They were much like he had always imagined them to be: beautiful beings, perfectly proportioned, robed in immaculate white gowns that were so bright, so radiant, they hurt his eyes—and yet he could not help but stare at them, could not break his gaze away from them.

And they spoke to him—spoke directly into his heart. Their sweet voices filled his mind with wonder and love, with awe and ecstasy.

Afterwards, it saddened him to have to leave the church, to leave the angels behind. And he felt great remorse, loss because he could not stay forever in their presence, and could recall only fragments of what they had told him.

Analysis of the First 1955 Encounter

Heriot's short story contains many mundane details of the 1950s trips beyond the key alien/paranormal elements, which suggests that, when he wrote it, he still retained clear and precise memories of the events. The beginning scenes are told from the mother's point of view and it is interesting to note that she was aware of Earl's distracted, other-worldly state of mind. "He seemed (. . .) to be lost in a daze (. . .) a dream world of his own (. . .) He wasn't completely with them. His mind wandered off (. . .) She imagined his soul just drifting off, out of the car, out over the desert, dissipating into the wide open spaces." In effect, she was thinking that he was very different from the other family members. By writing this, Earl implied that as a child he often lived in an altered state of consciousness, one that may have enabled him to perceive and at least partly recall incursions of beings from another dimension.

It's also worth noting that on this 1955 trip, Earl saw a giant insect—not once but twice. Is this a foreshadowing of the initial alien visitation coming later in the same trip, and does it hint that the aliens he saw—whose physical appearance he doesn't describe in any detail, other than saying they have ". . . horrible faces. Not the faces of men"—are in fact giant insect-like creatures? Two of Earl's alien sightings reported in *Little Gray Bastards* were of insect-like beings. In junior high school, during the period 1961 to 1962 (and possibly earlier in elementary school), he saw a Mantid alien. The junior high and elementary school Mantids were different heights and colors. Then, in college, sometime between 1966 and 1972, he saw a group of tan-gray insect-like aliens at a friend's apartment.

The basics of the first alien visitation described in "Little Church in the Pines" is that the family slept in their car at a truck turn-off along the highway in the Mojave Desert. In the early morning hours "they were visited." The incident began with the car being approached by lights—possibly from a UFO—that flooded the interior of the vehicle. Only Earl was awakened by the light; the rest of the family slept through it. He saw "dark figures in front of the light" (i.e., between him and the light source). The silhouetted alien figures, numbering at about a dozen, stared at him through the car windows and communicated with him by means of "foreign words that he shouldn't have understood, but did." However, the next morning he failed to remember the meaning of what they had told him. This communication appears to have been telepathic in nature rather than vocal speech; the aliens "words passed through the glass like radio waves, (. . .) straight into his (. . .) brain."

The next morning, there was no discussion among family members regarding the terrifying nocturnal event. It was as if it had never even happened.

Analysis of the Second 1955 Encounter

Earl's second encounter with non-human entities during the 1955 vacation trip occurred one week after the first one. By this point in their eastward trek, Earl wrote they were "half a continent away"—roughly 1,300 miles—and were no longer in the Mojave Desert but in a "cool green valley thick with forest" and still a day's drive away from his aunt's home, which Earl says was in the Chicago area. Given these admittedly vague details, I suspect they may have driven east from the Mojave to Missouri and then north through the Missouri River Valley towards Chicago, but that is merely speculation on my part.

As with the earlier alien encounter at a truck turn-off, this second visitation was preceded by a disturbing incident in which insects played a role: a bug-infested motel room. Again, I have to wonder if an appearance by insects somehow foreshadowed the arrival of aliens.

Then, one night after a few more days spent driving through forests, they couldn't find a space at a campground and resorted to sleeping in their car at a small town city park. This was where the second alien encounter occurred. At some point after midnight, Earl woke up, looked out the car's rear window, and saw a large group of backlit figures approaching. In "strange, foreign-sounding speech," the aliens urged him to leave the car and go off with them. He almost did as they asked, but ultimately resisted, in response to which their seemingly kind, persuasive tone changed to angry threats. By then, the creatures were so close that he saw their "thin elongated fingers" touching the car's windows and doors. Then, suddenly, they were gone, and the terrified Earl cried himself back to sleep. In the morning, Earl told his mother only that he had had a "bad dream." As before, the other family members had slept through the entire incident, and there was no mention of anything unusual having taken place during the night.

Comparison of the Two 1955 Encounters

Although these two incidents occurred far apart geographically and were separated in time by more than a week, they have a lot in common. In both cases, the family was sleeping in their car, and isolated from others. And in both cases, the entities approached from the direction of, and backlit by, a bright light. Furthermore, the entities communicated with Earl, apparently telepathically in both cases. They used what sounded to him like a foreign language, and yet he understood their intent, as if not only the sound but the meaning of the language had been transmitted directly into his mind.

Although for convenience I have been referring to these mysterious non-human beings as "aliens," in both cases there was no sighting of a UFO and no evidence to support the assumption that they were extraterrestrials. In both instances a number of these beings approached Earl during the early morning hours and, during the second visitation, attempted to lure him into leaving the relative safety of the parked car of his own free will. He did not give in to them and as far as can be determined by the text of "Little Church in the Pines," an abduction did not occur on either occasion. I have to wonder why these nocturnal visitors would need him to surrender himself up to them willingly. Couldn't they break into the car and take him against his will? Or is there something in the nature of the entities' relationship with humans—or with higher supernatural forces—that they must gain the subject's permission before certain actions can be taken? If that's the situation, it calls to mind the lore that there is a "rule" that says demonic forces must be invited into a home or into a person's life; they cannot simply force their way in.

Contrary to the idea that such a rule may be in effect, many abductees report that they have been taken entirely against their will, with no permission having been granted to the aliens to kidnap the person, perform medical procedures and tests, and subject them to what are often terrifying and unpleasant experiences. One explanation for this apparent inconsistency in the treatment of potential abductees is that different alien species may be interacting with humans, and that those species may operate under different protocols. Another possible explanation is that there are different classes of humans when it comes to their being available for abduction. Perhaps selected individuals have been pre-approved for abduction and are free game, so to speak, while others are of protected status and are off-limits, unless the person overtly agrees to participate in the abduction scenario. And who is it that would be granting this permission to abduct, or not, and enforcing such protocols? Human governments? Superior alien species? Higher spiritual forces? The aliens themselves in the context of their own ethical standards? For whatever reason, if the story told in "Little Church in the Pines" is complete, with nothing important omitted, Earl Heriot twice was able to ward off a full-blown alien abduction during the 1955 trip, although he did have frightening close encounters of the third kind.

Analysis of the 1957 Apparition of Angels

Two years later, in the summer of 1957, at the end of another vacation trip, Earl Heriot had what might be called a religious vision in a church set deep in the woods near his aunt's house in the Chicago area. During an evening service there he saw angels clustered around the altar. They appeared to be "Living (. . .) creatures (. . .) beautiful beings, perfectly proportioned, robed in immaculate white gowns that were so bright, so radiant, they hurt his eyes."

He not only saw them; he also heard them: "They spoke to him (. . .) directly into his heart. Their sweet voices filled his mind with wonder and love, with awe and ecstasy."

Although he interprets these beings as traditional angels, there are a couple similarities between this overwhelmingly positive experience and the decidedly negative encounters he had with non-human entities during the 1955 trip. In 1955, the "aliens" seemed to have emerged from out of a bright light, which may or may not have been a landed UFO, while in 1957, the "angels" appeared to radiate their own bright light. Could it be that in all three instances, the light, which is electromagnetic energy in wave form, was acting as a medium through which paranormal entities were entering our dimension?

The second similarity between Earl's 1955, and 1957, experiences is that in all three instances, the entities that Earl witnessed communicated with him. Like the aliens, the angels seem to have spoken to Earl telepathically, rather than through vocal speech. Earl says that he wanted to stay forever in the presence of these angelic beings, which is not all that different from what the aliens wanted of him: to go away with them forever. The relationship between the angels on one side, and the aliens on the other side, is the dichotomy between good and evil, and between beauty and ugliness. Would it be too much of a stretch to think that these two mutually exclusive categories of beings are in fact one and the same—merely the two opposing faces of the same phenomenon? In essence, is Earl being jerked around by paranormal forces and made to live through a false drama of "good" versus "evil"? It is suggestive of this possibility that Earl saw the angels in a situation that was much like the circumstances in which he previously saw the aliens: at night, in an unfamiliar setting, a long way from home. Was some devious non-human intelligence toying with his mind over a two-year period?

Saucer in a Pit

In *Little Gray Bastards*, Earl Heriot tells of a strange memory he has from childhood that may be related to the events described in "Little Church in the Pines," although Earl always thought of this as an isolated incident, unconnected to any of his other odd experiences, not having remembered the details of the 1955, and 1957, trips until he recently reread the story. The only context he has had until now for this strange childhood memory is that his family was on a vacation trip sometime in the 1950s or '60s, when he found himself "in a dense forest where there's a small flying saucer resting on the ground in a shallow circular pit." Although he has a fleeting memory of having been taken to the saucer and then of being inside of it, reclining on what looked like a dentist's chair, and having his left eye probed by a long needle-tipped instrument, he has no memory of having seen any beings—human or otherwise—during this event.

There's a strong possibility that this isolated "saucer in a pit" memory is part of the larger story of his 1955, and 1957, encounters. It's quite curious that his memories of the 1955, and 1957, incidents include non-human entities but no UFOs, while his memory of the 1950s–1960s "saucer in a pit" incident includes a UFO but no beings—human or otherwise. Perhaps his brain has compartmentalized the various elements in these experiences so as to protect his conscious mind from having to relive what may have been extremely traumatic abduction experiences.

It's as if he subconsciously decided to forget the scariest part—the presence of aliens—once he had recorded the events in "Little Church in the Pines" and has only allowed himself to consciously recall seeing and being inside the alien craft, which is bizarre in itself but not inherently terrifying.

Return of the Others

In *Little Gray Bastards* I told how Earl Heriot's nearly life-long pattern of having strange memories, thoughts, and experiences involving UFOs and aliens had lasted from the time he was about three years old, circa 1951, until the year 2000, when he was in his early fifties. Then, for unknown reasons, it stopped. Since his last UFO sighting in 2000, Earl had been enjoying his new-found freedom from the puzzling and often disturbing alien presence in his life, and he was not eager to have it return. Yet, return it did. In June 2015, Earl phoned me with news of a bizarre new experience, one he thought may have been a foiled alien abduction attempt. His upbeat tone during this call really took me by surprise, for by the time my initial investigation of Earl's case had wound down in 2014, he had grown weary of the subject, and was having second thoughts about the wisdom of going public with his story, even under the guise of a pseudonym. On top of which he was angry at me for having dredged up so many of his personal secrets, and was feeling very anxious and even paranoid about what might happen to him once the book came out. But listening to him in mid-2015, I could tell all that negative energy had evaporated. Now, he sounded excited and even a little awed that the mysterious phenomenon had once more entered his world.

"Hey," he said after we got the pleasantries out of the way, "I had a weird 'night terrors' thing while I was asleep about 4:00 a.m. this morning. I've had maybe ten similar experiences over the years, almost always at 2:00 or 3:00 a.m., but never this late in the morning. It always feels like I'm rushing forward through space at high speed, with a wind blowing in my face, but it may be more like an energy field or vibration. There's a loud roaring in my ears. My thought last night was *They're taking me!* Am I really ready to actually see these bastards? What will happen to me? I didn't see any aliens, but I felt a looming presence, as if they had suddenly appeared around me, and were accompanying me as I rushed forward. The experience ended a few seconds after I said a prayer, not out loud: *Bless and protect me, Lord Jesus Christ.* The roaring wind stopped and I suddenly felt totally calm and well. Using prayer as a way to stop abductions is something I read about years ago and it always seems to work. I think there are several ways to explain what happened. Maybe it was some type of minor seizure, a physiological thing. Or, maybe it was a release of stress; yesterday I was under a lot of pressure at work to quickly crank out a report. Or, maybe it was an abduction that was aborted by my calling on a higher power for protection. Then again, maybe I was in fact abducted, but my memory of everything but the beginning and end of the event was erased by the aliens. What do you think, David?"

"I think they're back."

"Seriously?"

"Seriously."

"Ha!" he said with strained laughter. "Maybe they are."

Summing up the Earl Heriot Case

As I've documented, throughout most of his life Earl Heriot has had a wide variety of uncanny memories, strange thoughts, and bizarre experiences pertaining to UFOs, aliens, and other related paranormal phenomena. He is at a loss to adequately explain any of it, and in particular to identify who or what is behind it. All he can do is relegate it to the unsatisfying category of "the unexplained."

You might expect that he would come away from all these experiences with a set of core beliefs or fundamental ideas that he has picked up from the visitors, or at least a deeper understanding of who they are, why they are here, and what they want from us, but he hasn't. On the occasions when he has seen what he thinks are aliens, they have generally not communicated with him. His 1955, and 1957, vacation encounters were exceptions to this rule, in that he remembers they did in fact speak to him—in an unrecognized language that he nonetheless understood—but the only content he later recalled from those communications was their attempt to lure him into going away with them to some unknown destination for unstated purposes. For all his experiences with these mysterious beings, there has not been a single instance when they have imparted any sort of message to him for his own personal benefit or the greater benefit of all humanity. The aliens have offered no insights regarding humanity's present difficulties and given no advice that might help guide us as we wrestle with our future challenges. They have told Earl absolutely nothing about themselves that he can remember. In a word, there has been no message from the aliens. Considering the totality of his UFO-related experiences, Earl can see no meaningful pattern from which he might draw conclusions about the aliens. His experiences seem to be haphazard and devoid of worthy intent on the part of the aliens. It is all noise and no signal.

Lacking any discernible message, meaning, or pattern, Heriot's lifetime of random weird experiences appears to have no purpose beyond the perverse satisfaction that aliens seem to derive from toying with human minds and emotions, and possibly, the collection of genetic material for their own purposes. Lacking good evidence to the contrary, it's not unreasonable to assume that they regard us as their playthings, a resource to be used and discarded. There are a number of experiencers who, unlike Earl, do report positive messages from aliens, but where are the good actions on the aliens' part that should accompany such benign messages? Are experiencers who report primarily positive encounters with aliens being grossly deceived? Are the lofty messages these sincere witnesses receive merely a clever distraction designed to conceal the aliens' less than noble real intentions? To better understand what the aliens are up to, perhaps we should examine not what they say but what they actually do—and unfortunately most of that is very unpleasant for anyone who is forced to live through it.

Earl Heriot and the Iteration of Memory

(by Jordan)

Unlike David, I have never met Earl Heriot. I know him only through his own words and David's retelling of Earl's truly bizarre life of high strangeness. I do not have any reason to doubt his personal stories. In fact, I have my own reasons for accepting that, in spite of all his uncertainty, Earl's experiences are for the most part truly recalled experiences. Why? Because his memories are a jumble of paranormal craziness thrown into a blender and pureed. If his stories followed a logical unveiling of mysterious events leading to greater understanding of the paranormal, I should have reason to doubt him. But there is a rough, uneven quality to the stories that lends them more credibility than a carefully told tale of well-considered and planned-out episodes. In short, I accept Heriot's stories because they make no damned sense.

Heriot is obsessive when it comes to his memories. He revisits strange events repeatedly, relives the past as if seeking out every crumb of experience down to the last microgram. Something that seems not to have occurred to Heriot is that memories themselves change with time. We are, as Hume states in his "bundle theory" of self, a collection of ill-remembered memory that creates and recreates a "person." Memory of recent events can prove shaky. Then there is the derivative of the memory of a memory, and so on. Through each iteration, memory of actual events becomes more and more unreliable. The lucky news from Heriot is that he has many of these memories recorded in written accounts, fiction, and poetry. This is the other reason I accept Heriot's autobiographical narrative as representative of some greater overarching truth that has intruded into the life of an American Everyman.

Earl Heriot is the personified paranormal experience: a narrative of stranger things that are dreamt of in non sequitur philosophies. And none of it makes any effing sense.

CHAPTER 5

CHAPTER 5
Welcome to Flat Water

(by Jordan)

> Strong evidence suggests that we are dealing with a phenomenon that is being caused by palpable, solid objects whose characteristics are not of human design, and whose behavior is suggestive of intelligent control.
>
> —Peter Davenport
> Director, NUFORC (National UFO Reporting Center)

Flat Water, USA, is a small town with a population of only 310 people, founded in 1880, as the official City of Flat Water. Its mineral soda springs were discovered in 1848, by Randal Crowe (he thought himself very ironic upon naming the future town Flat Water) who placed the center of town at the springs and sold its "medicinal waters" to white settlers. The town quickly flourished and grew, vying for position as state capital. It lost out as capital, but the soda spring's font was incorporated as the first state park in 1890. Ever since Flat Water's earliest inception its springs have brought visitors from near and far—and very far—away.

UFOs are often seen attracted to water, and many probably spend most of their time underwater as USOs (Unidentified Submerged Objects). They are also attracted to specific metals, minerals, and compounds, including aluminum, benitoite, boron, coal, copper, gold, gypsum, iron, lead, magnesium, manganese, mercury, molybdenum, petroleum, silver, sodium chloride, steel, sulfur, titanium, uranium, and zinc—and apparently soda springs too, which contain (at the minimum) dissolved carbon dioxide and thus carbonic acid, as well as calcium carbonate. UFOs have been witnessed hovering over the center of town, right above the mineral spring's font.

Recently, Flat Water was host to extraterrestrial visitation. The event was played out for five highly credible witnesses: Sharon (the Mayor of Flat Water), her husband, Gene (a police officer), and son, Lance (a fourteen-year-old ROTC student), and friends Carol (a public school teacher) and her husband, Barry (a City Councilman of Flat Water). From that sighting, an amazing photograph of five structured craft was obtained, along with a simultaneous video of one craft becoming two. Sharon's updated sighting report to MUFON follows:

> On January 1, 2016, 12:23 a.m., my husband and I witnessed three bright orange balls or spheres. Then on February 24, 2016, at 8:27 p.m., five of us witnessed the

same phenomenon. Only this time I had my phone and knew to take some pictures, regardless of how often space shots do not turn out. No one believed us last time [in January]. At least few would admit to believing us. This time, Carol had her phone recording the orange "balls." I only took two photos, giving up to watch instead. It was later that I enlarged the photos and saw the real deal!

The first time in January, my husband, Gene, saw an orange ball out in the clear, dark, cold night. I came outside to see what he was looking at—it seemed like an orange glowing fireball. We had trouble accepting what we were witnessing. We had just watched some fireworks twenty minutes earlier. So we tried to reason out an unexploded firework, or an airplane coming straight at us as we waited to see its blinking lights. That never happened. What did happen was the ball moved across the sky in a slow, deliberate pattern, similar to a figure eight. Then another of equal size came across the sky in a quicker motion to the other. They moved together in the same type of a pattern, yet apart. They were not touching. They were not that close to each other, but it felt like they were communicating. The second one moved farther away and a third appeared from the first one. It was smaller in size but not by much. All three moved around the sky, then the second moved in a straight line out and away. The third went in a deliberate downward angled direction toward town from where we were standing. The first went down some, then back away from us toward the west and disappeared. All three were gone.

The second time we witnessed this sighting, the small type of orange glowing fireballs, was on February 24, 2016, at 8:25 p.m. Again, my husband, Gene, first spotted it, along with my fourteen-year-old son, Lance. They called to us: Barry and Carol and myself. The ball was back! You could see it glowing in the night sky; there were no stars visible at that time. The sky was partially cloudy, very dark. And there was the fireball moving in the slow, deliberate pattern again. But only one. We watched for more and tried to make certain that, yes, it was really true. There was something out in the sky at a fairly close distance to us. It seems to me that they were right over Peeker's Butte, which is several miles away. I definitely would call it a UFO. Carol took a video of what we were seeing and what we could not see with the naked eye. I stared in wonder during her recording. We realized after a few minutes that at some point she had lost the object and focused on another light source.

After we went back inside, I looked at my pictures to see if I had gotten anything. And, OH MY GOODNESS, I had indeed. I captured two lights that were clearly not stars. The lower light to the right was a radio tower light, as we confirmed the next evening. The higher light on the left appears to be a spaceship. It looks exactly like the typical sightings of the UFO spaceships: a saucer. The light is clearly different from all the other patterns of artificial lights and the stars. These lights are too perfect in conformity not to be created by a being. Whether it be a human or what, this was created by a being. The next evening we tried to recreate the pictures I had taken when I was first outside to see it, at 8:27 p.m. At 8:30 p.m. on February 25, we took pictures of the night sky again; there were no stars in the same area, but I did take some shots of the radio tower that is on the Butte. That tower is in the pictures from the night before and should help determine the distance of where it was in our sky view. I did take several pictures of stars in the sky. The distance of the glowing UFO and the stars is incredibly different. The stars can barely be seen on a clear night sky.

Carol added her perspective as eyewitness of the February 24, encounter:

We had Sharon, Gene, and Lance over for dinner on February 24. When Gene went to take Lance home next door he saw an orange glowing light moving in the sky and called us all out to look at it. I started filming the big ball of orange fire with my phone video camera and Sharon was taking still pictures at the same time with her phone camera. The light was rocking back and forth and up and down, and I captured it on video. The upper left object separated into two objects, shot up into the sky, came back down, zoomed out and back into frame in a flash, and disappeared, shooting up and away. When I tried to find it in my camera again I focused in on a radio tower light and got really excited because I thought there were two, but after examining it I realized that the second time I had focused in I lowered my camera and possibly got the radio tower light. The first orange ball of light did not return, and the other object shot straight up and was gone. I went out the following night and tried to capture any stars or lights and could not recreate the video on my camera. When I first saw the light with my eyes, before I had it on video, it was a bright orange, fire-like ball and it was moving back and forth and up and down in a slow manner, then fast, then it would just stop. After I got it focused in on my video, I stopped watching it with my eyes and just concentrated on it with my video. We all knew that we were seeing something that wasn't man-made, like lanterns or an airplane, but extraterrestrial. I got the feeling that the UFOs knew they were being watched. It was almost heart-stopping when we magnified the photo and saw that the lights were definite saucer-shaped objects. I exclaimed, "Holy shit!" I'm worried that they will come back for me. They know that I know they're there. I know that they will be back.

You can hear the genuine wonder, awe, excitement, and possibly fear in Carol's voice as she shot video of the craft zipping about and splitting apart:

Alright, I've got it on camera. I'm filming it right now. It's definitely moving back and forth—can you guys see it on my camera? Look at how fast it's moving back—oop, there it goes. Can you see how fast it's going back and forth, you guys? I lost it—I can see it but I lost it in my frame. Shoot, I lost it in my frame. Why can't I see it now? There it is. I got it back. Two of them! Two of them, look! Two. Can you see both of them on my camera? They're still on my camera. They're going back and forth.

For most of the witnesses, this February event was not their first sighting of UFOs. Barry has seen them since he was twelve years old. He was traveling in the car with his parents in the desert when five balls of light crossed the road in front of their vehicle. Each was about the size of a basketball, kept pace ahead of the moving car for about a minute, stopped, seemed to communicate, and then were gone in a flash. He also recalls his parents witnessing a UFO hovering over Phoenix, Arizona, for about an hour back in the 1960s. Yet he has no real interest in UFOs or ufology in general.

Sharon and Gene have both had previous sightings. On July 4, 2015, Sharon and Gene were watching a fireworks display over Flat Water. At 10:45 a bright object, brighter and apparently closer than a mere satellite, was traveling north. In an instant it turned 180° and shot off across the sky south and disappeared. The entire sighting lasted about a minute. Sharon and Gene tried to rationalize what they had just seen. Surely the object they saw was a remnant of the fireworks or . . . but they were unable to convince themselves of such a prosaic explanation. They had no sense of communication from the object.

On New Year's Eve 2015, Barry and Carol watched fireworks over Flat Water with Gene, Sharon, and Lance. They were outside, facing Flat Water, when in the earliest moments of 2016. at 12:30 a.m., an orange ball appeared above the town and began a series of figure eight motions. Then from the left of the object another orange orb appeared and merged with the first one. The orb then split again, producing three objects. They moved erratically with sharp angle turns and high speeds, came back close together, headed west, and then all three objects shot off in different directions at incredible speed and disappeared. The sighting lasted four-and-a-half minutes. The objects were estimated to be approximately a quarter mile away from the witnesses at their closest. The objects spent most of their time directly above the mineral soda spring fountain in the center of town. There had been Chinese lanterns along with the fireworks, but these objects behaved like neither. The witnesses mentioned that the orbs seemed to be communicating with one another as they moved in unison to the west and then took off into the night.

Five saucers perform incredible feats and maneuvers over Peeker's Butte, approximately five miles from Flat Water. Craft magnified. *Photograph by Sharon Hawking, 2016.*

Next came the big sighting on February 24. Lance, Barry, and Gene first spotted a bright orange object five miles away over Peeker's Butte; Sharon and Carol soon joined them. The orb moved lower in the sky, rocking back and forth like a leaf on the breeze. For a while they only noticed the single orb, then two as the one divided. The rest of the sighting has been adequately described above. Carol reiterated, however, that she feels the objects will return, "without a shadow of a doubt."

The photo on page 73 that Sharon shot with her cell phone on February 24, clearly shows the two brightest objects on the left (an intense orange glow) and three more objects to the right (glowing white). The lights on the bottom are the tower lights on top of Peeker's Butte. When the objects are magnified, an immediately recognizable saucer-like dark shape can be seen around the "orbs," showing clearly the structured shape of the craft.

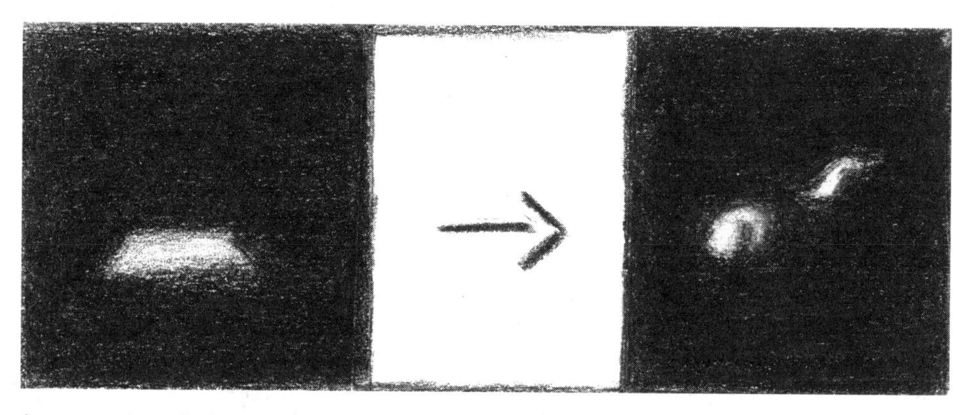

A saucer somehow splits into two "plasmas" and then each into two solid craft. *Graphite on paper, 5 ½" x 2", by Anna Hofer, 2016 (from low-resolution screen shots of video taken by Carol Langley, 2016).*

An analysis of Carol's video reveals the moment at which the two objects on the left in Sharon's photo split apart. There is a bar of horizontal light as the one craft becomes two and directly after that two spiral shapes. It appears as if the craft became a plasma, divided into two plasmas and then reformed into solid state. For about ten seconds the twin objects can be seen moving together as one object, one flashing off as the other flashes on, back and forth. The saucers that Carol captured on her phone appear white instead of orange, due to the difference between the aperture in Carol's phone and that in Sharon's. The still frames do not have high enough resolution for printing, but the graphite illustrations above are accurate.

The object on the far right of Sharon's photograph, when enlarged, clearly displays the shape of the craft. It is not, in fact, a "classic saucer" but a saucer shape with projections out the front and rear of the craft. The magnification was not high enough resolution but, again, the graphite illustration on the next page above (and the LEGO model below) is accurate to the photo enlargement.

The saucers' physical shape is captured in the furthest craft to the right (on page 73). *Graphite on paper, 3" x 2 ¾", by Anna Hofer, 2016 (from low-resolution magnification of photo taken by Sharon Hawking, 2016).*

Model of the Flat Water craft reconstructed by Jordan Hofer using LEGO Digital Designer, 2016. *Photograph by Jordan Hofer, 2016.*

I do not have access to 3D printing, so I used an old standby: LEGO Digital Designer (LDD). This tool allowed me to build the model on the screen and then order the parts to construct it. I also used LDD to rotate the model in three dimensions. No matter how you turn the model, as long as the light on the bottom of the craft is oriented to the eye, you can recreate all of the "saucer" shapes in the photograph. The final physical LEGO model is shown above with a white bar on the bottom representing the intense white glow of the object on the far right in Sharon's photograph.

How large are the craft? I was able to calculate the line of sight distance from the witnesses in Flat Water to the objects over Peeker's Butte and came up with a little more than five miles. Carol says each of the craft was about the size of a 747.

Why are UFOs attracted to Flat Water? The town's mineral springs may offer an answer. What's in it, aside from carbon dioxide and carbonic acid, that might be attracting UFOs? The water testing report for Flat Water was a report of what is not in the mineral springs: no nitrates, copper, or lead. Common minerals in soda springs include calcium and magnesium. The Flat Water 2015 Annual Drinking Water Quality Report gives an exhaustive list of possible contaminants:

> As water travels over the surface of the land or through the ground, it dissolves *naturally occurring minerals* and, in some cases, *radioactive material*, and can pick up substances resulting from the presence of animals or from human activity: microbial contaminants, such as viruses and bacteria, that may come from sewage treatment plants, septic systems, agricultural livestock operations, and wildlife; inorganic contaminants, such as *salts and metals*, which can be naturally occurring or result from urban storm water runoff, industrial, or domestic wastewater discharges, *oil and gas production*, mining, or farming; pesticides and herbicides, which may come from a variety of sources such as agriculture, urban storm water runoff, and residential uses; organic Chemical Contaminants, including synthetic and volatile organic chemicals, which are by-products of industrial processes and *petroleum* production, and can also come from gas stations, urban storm water runoff, and septic systems; and *radioactive contaminants*, which can be naturally occurring or be the result of oil and gas production and mining activities. [*Emphasis added.*]

UFOs are attracted to the contaminants italicized above, especially radioactive material. Minerals, salts and metals, and petroleum products also attract UFOs. Yet I doubt it is only minerals, etc., that are calling the saucers. Something else is occurring, and I doubt I will ever divine it.

Shortly after first receiving the sightings report I spoke with Peter Davenport, Director of the National UFO Reporting Center (NUFORC), at the UFO Festival in McMinnville, Oregon. After describing the craft and their color to Peter, he told me that he had been inundated by reports of these "orbs," as they appear to the naked eye:

> I mentioned the number of reports of red, orange, and yellow "orbs" that had been collected over the past four years. I have posted approximately 200 to 300 such reports per month, for the last 48 months . . . roughly 10,000 to 15,000 such reports, over that four-year period (Email correspondence, June 2, 2016).

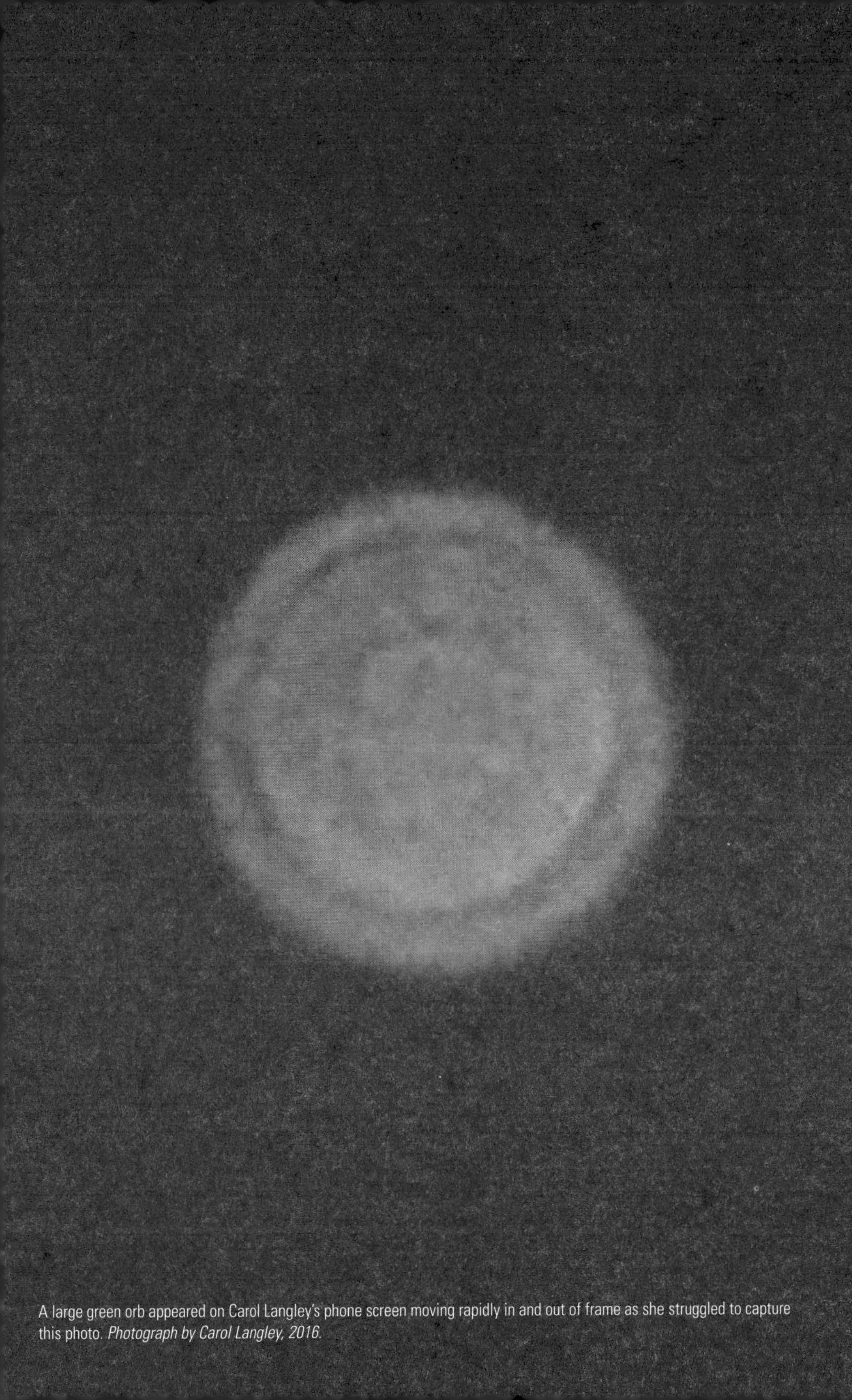

A large green orb appeared on Carol Langley's phone screen moving rapidly in and out of frame as she struggled to capture this photo. *Photograph by Carol Langley, 2016.*

My daughter mentioned her sighting of a red orb in 2013, and realized a peculiar irony: 15,000 is the same number as all the Garfield comics over the last thirty-nine years—just for perspective. Peter Davenport is a very dedicated man! I definitely got the sense that he thought this onslaught of orb reports might be indicative of some unknown impending event (In conversation, May 12, 2016). That was an ominous moment for me.

Then, on July 2, 2016, Carol and Barry were watching a fire in the distance. Carol was shooting photos of the fire when an object appeared on her phone's screen that she could not see with the unaided eye.

> We were watching a fire on the horizon at 11:30 p.m., which just ended up turning out to be a big bonfire, and I was pointing my camera towards it, and this big green thing kept coming into the frame and going out. I was finally able to snap a picture of it, but we couldn't see it at all in the sky! What in the world do you think this could be? Compared to the lights in the background, this was huge. It came across my frame quickly from left to right and disappeared. I tried to follow it and I got it back in my frame and it went up . . . but it was fast moving and kept going back and forth. Barry kept hollering to snap a pic, but I only was fast enough to get one then it was gone . . . if we were to actually see it with our eyes, it seems that it would have been right in our field in front of my house. There was no noise. The city lights would look like a tiny pinprick of light next to it.

Another orb to add to Peter Davenport's deluge? The orb was very close to Carol and Barry, but they could not see it without the enhanced vision of the camera. It does not look at all like a lens flare but appears to be what it is: a green orb. No light sources present could have caused a lens flare, and this "lens flare" moved rapidly, and its source was invisible to the human eye! Upon viewing the photo I am convinced the orb is alive. It is even strikingly reminiscent of a cell, with its outer ring as the cell membrane and the green inside as chlorophyll. I do not believe this literally, but all of my biological schooling, researching and teaching leads me to the conclusion that the orb is alive. Carol's premonition that the UFOs would return turned out to be correct. I recommended she contact NUFORC and add a straw to Peter's back.

The sightings have not left the Flat Water witnesses unaffected. Carol says that her worldview has changed, and Sharon even argues for the existence of extraterrestrials. Fourteen-year-old Lance simply does not want to accept what he saw. The objects were not stars, planets, satellites, fireworks, Chinese lanterns, airplanes, helicopters, balloons, or drones—they were UFOs, structure known but unidentifiable. Now what remains to be seen is whether more craft will soon return. The frustration lies in the waiting. But if Peter Davenport's sense of an impending incident is correct, none of us may have long to wait.

David's Common Pie Problems

Jordan's analysis of the Flat Water UFO case is based on the report that Sharon, the town's mayor, made to MUFON, his subsequent conversations with her by email and phone, his technical analysis of photos and video captured during the February 24, 2016, sighting, and an in-person interview with the four adult witnesses that Jordan and I conducted on the evening of June 4, 2016.

I was somewhat surprised when Jordan informed me that the witnesses had asked to meet with us to discuss their multiple sightings. Jordan had already told me that, like most people who have a UFO sighting, the witnesses are not seeking publicity. While millions of Americans (about ten percent of the population according to recent polls) have reported seeing things in the skies that they cannot explain away as mundane objects such as stars, planets, conventional aircraft, birds, insects, clouds, etc., there remains a deep-seated bias in our culture against UFOs, and the average person is hesitant to express an interest in the subject. The topic is almost universally considered tainted, even toxic, and anyone who publicly states that they believe in UFOs or claims to have seen one is subject to ridicule both privately in their personal life and publicly by the news media. For most people, this fact alone is enough to compel them to keep silent about what they've seen. Others, who are unusually brave or thick-skinned, may initially openly talk about their sighting(s), but often they soon come to regret having done so when they are called "crazy," "liar," or "hoaxer" by co-workers, friends, and even family members. Given this dreadful social intolerance towards what is becoming a fairly common experience shared by many people all over the world, I would expect any UFO observer to be reluctant to meet with strangers to discuss their experience. But the Flat Water observers aren't your run-of-the-mill UFO witnesses. The four adult witnesses in this case are highly credible, mature, responsible individuals who are nothing less than community leaders in their town. Given this, they are even more vulnerable to ridicule than the average citizen if they express unconventional ideas or claim to have observed extraordinary, unexplained phenomenon. Simply put, they can little afford to talk about this subject openly. I can fully appreciate why they do not want to go public with their sightings. And yet, they feel it is important to share what they have experienced, and they want to get their story out there. That is why they agreed to let us write about their case, on the condition that we use pseudonyms to conceal their identity.

Jordan invited me to join him in the interview and I leaped at the chance. Arrangements were made for us to meet at a Denny's restaurant along the freeway near a small town that's a long ways from both Flat Water and the city where Jordan and I live. I have to admit that I was a bit nervous beforehand. Not because I'm shy about meeting people or speaking before a group—I'm not—but because I was apprehensive for the witnesses, anticipating that they might feel awkward, even embarrassed to be discussing something as bizarre as UFOs with strangers in a public place. I hoped they would feel at ease, that they would trust that we would be open-minded and respectful, and not judge them unfairly. And I hoped Jordan and I would appear competent and professional, and that we would be able to put them at ease.

The meeting was set for 7:00 p.m. on a Saturday. The chosen Denny's restaurant was too far for us to make the round trip drive in a single day, so Jordan and I decided we would turn it into a two-day road trip accompanied by his daughter, Anna. We set out early on Saturday morning, drove all day, and met the witnesses in another state on Saturday evening. This location was feasible for the witnesses because they happened to be on a joint vacation trip, far from their own home state. They said the Denny's was about an hour's drive, one way, from where they were camping. After the meeting was concluded, Jordan, Anna, and I found a nearby motel where we spent the night, and then we drove back home to Oregon on Sunday.

Jordan did the driving on Saturday, with Anna in the back seat and me riding shotgun. We over-estimated the time needed for the trip and arrived a half-hour early. That was a good thing because it gave us time to calm our minds and prepare mentally for the interview. It had been a very hot day, and the air outside was stifling as we got out of Jordan's air conditioned car, but inside Denny's it was cool. We explained to the waitress who showed us to our table that we were being joined by four others who should arrive soon. She asked if we wanted anything to drink while we waited for our guests. I asked for decaf coffee while Jordan wanted a Diet Coke and Anna wanted ice water. The waitress brought our drinks and left a stack of menus for us and the others to come. Studying the menu, we soon realized that almost everything on it featured bacon. There was even bacon in one of the ice cream sundaes. What I did not see was pie of any kind. Not even pie with bacon in it. We were stunned by this omission. When the waitress came by a few minutes later to check on us, I asked her if they had any pie.

"No," she said, "I'm sorry. For some reason, they took it off the menu. I don't know why."

As silly as it sounds, this was a profound disappointment to me. I had a mental image of drinking coffee and eating pie while we interviewed the witnesses about their UFO sightings. It just seemed like the right snack for the occasion. All the way there in the car I had my mouth set on that pie. What I hadn't yet decided on was whether I would go with apple or cherry, but I knew it would be a traditional choice along those lines. I got the idea for pie from the 1990s television series *The X-Files* and *Twin Peaks*. In both programs, characters eat pie in the midst of strange and mysterious circumstances.

"Why on Earth wouldn't they serve pie?" I asked Jordan after the waitress had left.

He was as puzzled as I. "I have no idea. It's crazy!"

"Maybe they had to take pie off the menu because they were having some sort of trouble with it," I speculated.

"What kind of trouble can you have with pie?"

"I don't know: common pie problems," I answered.

The absurdity of this phrase along with our nervousness about the meeting going well made us both crack up hysterically, snorting and guffawing wildly as we rattled off examples of common pie problems that might afflict a restaurant, such as flies buzzing around uncovered pies, crusts drying out and getting hard, fillings going bad, all because not enough people were ordering pie these days and they were sitting around uneaten. And these common pie problems would be exacerbated by the public's expectation that new pies would be baked fresh daily, only to go bad while waiting for someone to order a slice.

It seemed ridiculous to me that Denny's would stop serving a standard item like pie. Far more incredible than the idea that non-human intelligent beings from some unknown place or dimension would enter our airspace and be observed by humans.

This would be a terrible time for the witnesses to arrive, I thought. "If they see us like this, they'll think we're lunatics," I said. Thankfully we settled down after a minute and stopped laughing about pie problems, common or otherwise. Instead we talked about what we would ask them, and how we would do our best to avoid leading the witnesses. We would simply let them tell their story, ask basic questions and jot down their answers. We each had a notebook and a pen at the ready. Beforehand, we had talked about possibly recording the conversation, but decided that might be too intimidating to the witnesses, so we settled for only taking notes.

So why do I bring up the "no pie" situation at Denny's? How does that possibly belong in a discussion of an interview about UFOs? I do so because it serves to highlight the degree to which our perceptions about the world we live in—including ideas we might have about UFOs and aliens—are shaped by the media: films, TV, and mainstream news. And even though I'm a serious student of ufology and see myself as someone who thinks outside the box, when push comes to shove and I'm headed for a meeting where we'll talk about UFOs, I suddenly want coffee and pie. That's the media influence at work, and it shapes our ideas of who or what aliens are, so that more often than not, people who see a UFO believe they are observing a spaceship piloted by visiting extraterrestrials, because that's almost always the storyline in films, TV, and news accounts. Well, I didn't get any pie, but I did have a bowl of delicious broccoli and cheddar soup, along with two cups of decaf. Everyone else at the table—when our guests had arrived and we all ordered—had better instincts than I, given the heat, and wisely indulged in ice cream sundaes. Barry was the boldest of all, ordering the Maple Bacon Sundae. I also bring up what we ate because it proves something that I suspected the moment I met Carol, Barry, Sharon, and Gene; that they are normal, average people who just happened to see something truly strange and mysterious, and not once but several times. Like millions of Americans throughout this land, they have the good sense to eat ice cream on a hot evening. They are, in every way, just like the rest of us, and they have seen UFOs with their own eyes, and taken photos and videos of them that may enlighten the rest of us who are not so fortunate—or unfortunate—as to see these unknown objects for ourselves.

One other thing I want to mention before I get into the interview itself is an odd experience that happened beforehand. I went to the men's restroom a few minutes prior to the witnesses' arrival. Like I said, I was feeling a bit nervous, and unfortunately the trip to the restroom only heightened my unease. I always find public restrooms kind of eerie when I'm the only person in them. In this case, that feeling was made worse by the music that was audible throughout the restaurant but was much louder in the restroom. It was a bizarre instrumental version of the pop song, "Angel of the Morning," in which each "line" (had there been lyrics) ended with a long, drawn out electronic squeal that sounded like a small animal was being abused. It was so odd and so unpleasant that I could hardly believe it was actually being used as mood music by a major restaurant chain. There I was, far from home, in an older, somewhat funky Denny's, and a demonic version of "Angel of the Morning" was playing in the abandoned restroom. That song, in that tortured version, in the context of meeting with strangers to discuss UFOs, really creeped me out. I wondered to myself if this were some sick joke being played on me by the Grays. Maybe the message that was being delivered by the song is that they, materializing in bedrooms in the early morning hours as they do, are angels of the morning, so to speak. I did my business and got out of there as fast as possible.

Jordan has fully discussed the physical aspects of the sightings, so I'll describe my subjective impressions of the witnesses—the human side of the story, so to speak. As I said previously, the witnesses struck me as highly responsible, no-nonsense people—community leaders, down-to-earth, regular Americans—and I liked them right away. They seemed honest, open, sincere, and trustworthy. Everything they told us—and they all joined in, each providing details from his or her own perspective—felt genuine. There were no false notes, and I never felt like they were exaggerating, or bending the truth. I'm convinced they saw exactly what they told us they saw on those three occasions. Their stories all agree, and they all appear to believe that what they saw was truly unexplained, unless the explanation is that they had seen artificial flying objects that were under the control of non-human intelligent beings.

That said, I had the strong impression that this was primarily Sharon and Carol's story. That the women "owned" the story, and the men (Barry and Gene) were just going along on the interview to support the women, both in terms of moral support and by offering their own testimony. The women seemed to have intense emotions about what they had experienced, while the men appeared to be more matter-of-fact about the whole thing. Now, this "impression" may all be in my mind. I may simply be perceiving the normal dynamics of couple-hood and projecting typical gender roles upon the witnesses. Perhaps the things I'm sensing are not actually in the witnesses' minds. Be that as it may, I had the feeling that if the men alone had seen the UFOs, and not the women, we wouldn't have been meeting. My impression was that the men would take the experience of seeing UFOs in stride, absorb the new information as part of their larger view of how the universe works, but for the women, their entire view of life had been changed by the sightings.

Interestingly, Sharon and Carol seemed to relate differently to the phenomenon they had both observed. Sharon said that she had seen strange, unexplained things in the sky all her life, in Flat Water and in other places she had lived. In contrast, the February 2016 sighting was Carol's first observation of UFOs. She said it "changed my view of everything, forever." The sightings led Sharon to believe that extraterrestrials really do exist and are present in our world.

The women appear to have different emotional reactions to the sightings. Sharon said that at first she had told a few people what she had seen, but "they didn't believe me." Since then, she has stopped telling people. The reaction of disbelief from people she confided in has given the subject a negative tone for her. She seems to regret having told anyone about it. She also seems to have some fear regarding the UFOs. "I'm not sure I want to find out what is out there," is how she put it.

In comparison, Carol has a largely positive attitude about the UFOs. She described the February 2016 sighting as "the most fun" of the three sightings because they all saw it, and finally, she and Barry could believe what Sharon and Gene had been telling them all along. Unlike Sharon, Carol doesn't care if people don't believe her when she talks about the sightings. She goes right on telling people about it. Carol had the feeling that the February 2016 sighting wouldn't be the last time she would see the UFOs. "It's like a feeling in my heart. There's not a shadow of a doubt that they were coming back." She seems excited by the prospect of further sightings.

I came away from the interview with a heightened sense of the profound gulf that separates the fragile and limited minds of the human witnesses and whatever superior intelligence may be operating through the medium of the phenomenon that, for convenience, we call a "UFO sighting." The modern UFO era began seven decades ago and yet we still know so very little about what is actually happening when a person sees a UFO or interacts with an alien being. We can't say for certain if the things being reported by credible witnesses like Sharon, Gene, Carol, and Barry are purely physical creatures in mechanical ships, or supernatural entities in phantom craft that exist only for the duration of the sighting, or a combination of the physical and the paranormal—tangible demons who lurk in the darkest depths of our troubled dreams as much as they hail from remote regions of the starry skies. Clearly, there is some form of intelligence behind the UFO phenomenon, but we can't be certain there is any form of consciousness inherent in that intelligence. In other words, for all we know, these "aliens" may be soulless artificial cyborgs, and "there's nobody home" as the saying goes. Listening to the Flat Water witnesses tell their stories, seeing their faces and sensing the emotions behind their words, it was driven home to me just how fully human they, and all UFO witnesses, are. But as for the beings that pilot the ships they see, we can say nothing about their minds, their hearts, nor their souls—if they have any. It is all absurd theater on a cunningly lit stage, and we are the audience, but for what purpose? The Flat Water witnesses hope to learn more about what they saw and at least partly to understand it someday. I wish I could say they will achieve that, that we all will come to better understand it, but I'm not confident that will ever come to pass. So far, the UFO phenomenon remains largely unknown, and seemingly unknowable.

Jordan's Postscript: A Flat Water Flap

It would appear that the Flat Water area might be experiencing a UFO flap. Something very strange occurred on July 10, 2016, in the city of Banolan and was reported to MUFON on July 14, Case # 74271:

> Something traversed between my wife and I about four feet off the ground that made an unidentifiable noise and the speed of which was extraordinarily fast. Neither of us place any credence in "aliens among us" or visitations. My career was in astronomy on top of Mauna Kea in Hawaii. My wife was a banker and accountant. Whatever it was created a distortion in the air between us for an instant. We live in a suburban area, and our residence is surrounded by a fir forest. To the right of me from whence "it" came is a 150-meter-tall hill about 50 meters away, which we also own. Aside from the noise of the event there was absolutely no report one might ascribe to the discharge of a firearm. Our area is for the most part

dead quiet. If it were a bullet, etc., "it" would have to be able to climb a 150-meter-tall hill, go over the top, and then descend to our level and go absolutely parallel to the ground between us. I have been reluctant to report this because of my own core beliefs; however, one of my friends encouraged me to do so anyway. I have a home observatory (a Meade 12-inch LX200) and do a lot of observing and hunting for NEOs. I have yet to see anything unexplainable either here or on top of Mauna Kea. Having said that, the event my wife and I witnessed not only frightened us, but left us with profound curiosity as to its origin. The distortion in the air between us looked as if we were looking through water. The noise was subtle, but unlike anything we have ever heard. I own guns and know a ricochet when I hear one. Am I alone in this?

No description of an object was given because no object was seen. But whatever it was must have been hot enough to distort the atmosphere. Something very hot. A plasma, perhaps? Or was space-time itself distorted by the gravity drive of an invisible orb?

Then, in August 2016, I received the following query from Sharon: "What is this?" The email had a photo attached.

I zoomed over the bright spots in the photo, but only the one in the center had any form to it. And it was immediately, chillingly recognizable. "It's one of your saucers flipped on its side!" I replied excitedly.

"Oh, and that's exactly what I thought it was. Almost hoping it wasn't. After reading your books . . . lol," she replied, a little whistled tune through the graveyard.

"When did you see this? What's the story?"

Return of the UFO. The brightest light source in the center of the photograph is a craft flipped on its side. *Photograph by*

"We saw this last night, August 9, at 10:10 p.m. while standing in the Langleys' front yard, watching the sky. Dang close to the same flight pattern as last 4th of July [2015]. Fairly low, no sound, it came toward us, curved away and around, then disappeared. The same five of us [Sharon, Gene, Lance, Carol, and Barry] witnessed this UFO."

"I really think these sightings are somehow linked to you and Carol, especially," I ventured David's speculation.

"It could be the attraction to Gene," she replied. "He and I have seen them all. Carol has not. She and I do the reporting. It's interesting they've all been seen from my and Gene's homestead. Let me know your thoughts."

"Fascinating. So it's you and Gene to whom you feel the craft are attracted? Something about the location of your home, maybe? Did you receive the [abduction] questionnaire I sent you earlier?"

"We all feel it's the location. We read through the questionnaire and nothing in it rings true for any of us."

"That's good to hear," I said, "that the questionnaire does not apply to you. The next level is no fun for anyone. Okay, so if it's the location, do you have an idea of what's special about Flat Water to attract these things? I think you already know my speculation that it's the springs that are attracting the craft."

"Right?! It has to be the minerals in the water. The place was known for its healing waters. All the septic systems made the water unsafe to drink, but it's still here."

Just how long have saucers been attracted to Flat Water? Unfortunately, the story begins late for us in 2015, but the mineral springs have been in Flat Water long before the first European stomped on this continent.

Then Carol and Barry saw a UFO but not in Flat Water. Carol sent me an email with a photo attached.

"My husband and I went to a family reunion in [a neighboring state] this weekend and, as we were standing outside, that exact same light flew over the top of us in the same flight pattern and at the same altitude and completely disappeared right before our eyes. I did snap a picture of it; however, my camera is not nearly as good as Sharon's camera is . . . I don't know what the heck's going on but it's kind of freaking me out! I thought I would send the pic to you and get your thoughts. I feel like I'm being followed . . ."

I replied, "The white bar of light is what gives it away, and when I zoom in, I can see the object's shape. And yes, it does appear to be one of your saucers. Try not to freak out—I know, this coming from the man who's never seen a UFO! You are having some kind of contact, and it appears not to be restricted to Flat Water. I don't know what the heck's going on. Just keep snapping photos. The proof just keeps mounting."

"We saw this in [location hidden] (hot springs resort) last night, 13 of August, during our family reunion around 9 p.m. It was dark, and Barry and I were standing outside, and we looked up and saw it. I snapped a picture before it vanished, and I said, hey, that's the exact same light we saw in Flat Water! I showed him the pic Sharon got and we tried to compare the pictures. It was the highest resolution I could get . . . my phone camera sucks! I see the bar of light but I don't see any shape around it at all myself.

"Just a couple of notes that I find interesting," she continued. "When we saw the light over our land in Flat Water, it was flying lower in altitude than any of the airplanes that we saw that night. When the airplanes flew over we could hear their engines crystal clear. When this light flew over, we could not hear a thing, and it faded right before our eyes, unlike the airplanes . . . In [location hidden] last night it was the same thing . . . just a steady glowing light traveling rather slowly at a low altitude with no noise and faded into the sky right before our eyes on a crystal clear night."

I was pretty certain that the Flat Water UFOs were attracted to the town by the mineral springs, and Sharon was convinced that the UFOs were not interested in her and Carol. Now I have to wonder. There is a possible connection aside from the witnesses in the out-of-state sighting. Carol did mention that they were visiting a hot springs resort. Is there something in the water that is common to both locations? And if so, how frequent are UFOs at the out-of-state hot springs? Because if it's not the water, it must be the two families, Sharon's and Carol's. If the UFOs are initiating a form of contact, what message are they trying to convey?

I doubt the Flat Water story is over. And I doubt it will ever make sense.

A UFO follows Carol and family to a nearby state, hundreds of miles from Flat Water. *Photograph by Carol Langley, 2016.*

CHAPTER 6

CHAPTER 6
It's All Relative

(by David)

Over the course of his life, Earl Heriot has experienced both UFO-related events, including UFO sightings and alien encounters, and more "Earthly" paranormal phenomena involving ghosts and poltergeists that do not appear to be—at least overtly—associated with aliens. The same can be said of his family members. Like Earl, other members of the Heriot clan have had a number of UFO sightings, a few alien encounters, and diverse "non-alien" paranormal incidents. My focus has largely been on the UFO and alien events, rather than on the more general paranormal events. As interesting as some of the paranormal experiences are, they are unfortunately outside the scope of this book. In this chapter, I discuss the UFO experiences of Earl Heriot's family members, including his parents, his children, his older brother, Bud, who also goes by the nickname "Rooster" (both pseudonyms) and Bud's son, Andy (also a pseudonym).

It is often stated that alien abductions run in families. A common theory explaining this trend is that aliens are studying human genetics and performing genetic experiments on humans. By following the members of individual families over many generations, the aliens are able to determine the results of their genetic tinkering with human DNA. The larger purpose behind such experiments may be that they are part of a human-alien hybrid breeding program in which DNA from humans is mixed with alien genetic material, resulting in hybrid offspring bearing selected characteristics of both species: the Grays (of all alien species, the most likely to be involved in the hybrid breeding program) and humans. This theory goes a long way towards explaining the Grays' widely reported fascination with the reproductive systems and intimate relationships of their human subjects. Another commonly held view is that alien abductions run in families because people with certain physiological characteristics in their makeup are either more susceptible to being abducted in the first place or are more able to perceive aliens during abduction events and afterwards more likely to remember what they have experienced.

Mom's Little Men

Earl Heriot may have inherited his tendency for having consciously recollected alien encounters from his mother. When he was a child in the late 1950s or early 1960s, his mother had a disturbing nightmare in which she awoke in the middle of the night to find the bed surrounded by "little men." The dream—if that's what it was—was so unsettling that she was still quite distraught the next morning and needed to be comforted by his father. While the incident was explained to Earl and his brothers as being "only a bad dream" by their father, Earl suspected at the time that there was more to it, that it may have been real to some degree. His mother's story of a nocturnal bedroom visit by small humanoids is not all that different from Earl's own memories of being awakened in the middle of the night when the car the family was sleeping in was approached by mysterious figures on two occasions during a vacation trip made during the mid- to late-1950s. In addition to these suspected close encounters with alien beings, Earl's parents also had two noteworthy UFO sightings in the 1950s or 1960s, which are described in *Little Gray Bastards*.

Rooster and the Purple Orbs

Bud "Rooster" Heriot, who is three years older than Earl, has had a number of UFO sightings and odd, unexplained paranormal experiences over the years. In 1984, Rooster had a daylight sighting of a group of flying purple orbs that he watched for a few minutes from the window of his second-floor apartment in the Northwest district of downtown Portland, Oregon. I recall visiting him a couple times at that apartment. The building was located immediately west of the 405 Freeway, near W. Burnside Street. I should mention that I've known Rooster and his family for as long as I've known Earl Heriot, and I first heard about most of their UFO-related incidents shortly after they happened, but for each story that I share here, I've recently interviewed the witness (Rooster or his son) about it because I don't trust my memory when it comes to the details of something that I was told decades ago.

Rooster says he first noticed the unusual aerial objects as they approached from out of the southwest. They were four or five blocks away, floating like balloons at low altitude over the city, and were headed in a northeasterly direction. When he next paid attention to them, they were over the apartment building across the street from his and were less than 200 feet away. The objects were basically spherical in shape, although they were slightly taller than they were wide, and were about three feet across. There were six or seven of them in the group. The balloon-like orbs moved in unison, their position to one another remaining fixed, and they made no sound. The objects slowly passed by the window where he was standing. When he went to another window where he should have been able to see them again, given the path they were on, the objects were gone.

There are two reasons why Rooster is confident that they could not have been conventional balloons. The first reason is that the group of objects moved against the wind, which indicates they were under their own power and not being blown along by the wind like a balloon would be. The second reason is that they moved "in lock step"—as one—whereas hot air or helium-filled balloons would have moved independently, randomly changing their positions relative to one another. Beyond that, he didn't see any "tie off strings" such as balloons would have.

This wasn't Rooster's first UFO sighting. About 1976, he was working as a taxi cab driver in the city of Corvallis, Oregon. He claims that one night while he was driving the cab down Western Boulevard in Corvallis, he spotted a "giant white disc" in the sky over an A & W restaurant. The sighting was very brief, lasting only two seconds, so he didn't have time to judge the circular object's actual size or its distance from him. What he did notice is that it was the relative size (angular size) of the moon, and that it had what he described as "white flames behind it." The object was moving to the west when it disappeared. Currently, A&W does not have any restaurants in Corvallis, so presumably this location closed sometime after Rooster's sighting.

Rooster has never had the kinds of strange close encounters with alien beings that Earl claims to have had.

Andy's Purple Bolt of Light

Rooster's son, Andy, had a dramatic close encounter with a UFO when he was a boy. I recall hearing a very abbreviated account of this incident from Rooster in the early 1980s. The story I heard then was that Andy was home alone one night and saw a bright purple light shining down on the house from above. I don't see Andy very often, especially now that he's a grown man with a demanding job and a busy family life, and I never had a chance to ask him about it firsthand until we met at a social event in late July 2016. At that event I interviewed him in depth about his experience and what he told me follows.

The year was 1982 or 1983, and Andy was twelve or thirteen years old. At that time, Rooster and his family lived in an isolated two-story house out on US Route 20, the Corvallis-Newport Highway, which runs from Corvallis in Oregon's Willamette Valley, through the Coast Range, and to Newport on the coast, a distance of just under fifty miles. The house—which is no longer standing—was situated on a lonesome stretch of Route 20 a few miles northwest of the small town of Eddyville. The area is rural, heavily wooded, hilly, and remote with homes few and far between. Andy says the weird event happened in the fall—probably October or November. He remembers the season because it was during a part of the year when it started getting dark early. There was no lighting along the highway, and outdoor lighting of any kind around homes was minimal. I drove that road at night several times in the 1980s and it was pitch black outside of the beam of the car headlights. Andy claims he was at home alone—Rooster and his wife had not yet come home from work, and his younger sister, Tammy (a pseudonym), was off somewhere. At about 7:00 p.m., he suddenly felt "a strong presence" as if something had arrived outside, and "the dog went nuts," barking and jumping. He ran to a window and saw light coming down from above, but did not see an object. Then a shaft of very bright purple light slowly came down out of the sky from the direction of a glowing purple luminescence (presumably where the UFO was hovering) and hit the home's driveway, and then it went back up at the same angle, retracing its path. The light was very intense and had distinct edges; it was like a "bolt" of light or a cylinder made of light, in that it wasn't a continuous beam but had front and back edges. These bizarre strikes of slow moving, bright purple light happened two or three times, each time spanning about two minutes. During this activity, he could feel a "strong energy in the air," like static electricity, and he had the sense that "something was out there," above the house. He says he should have gone outside and looked for it, but he didn't—and he doesn't know why. He claims he was more excited than frightened and was actually disappointed when his parents came home and the UFO event abruptly ended as the lights disappeared. He thinks the entire episode lasted around five minutes. That was the only strange experience he ever had when they lived near Eddyville and his only UFO sighting until recently. Ironically, he didn't actually see a UFO that evening, but he doesn't know what else it could have been besides a UFO. It definitely was not a helicopter shining down a searchlight. He easily would have heard the loud noise of a helicopter's rotating blades given the absolute quietness of the environment out there. A UFO is his only good explanation. Would Andy have been abducted by aliens had his parents not shown up when they did? I think that's a strong possibility.

That is the event as remembered by Andy some thirty-four years later. Two weeks after my interview with Andy, I asked Rooster what he recalled about that night. Predictably, he mentioned the purple light, which is the main feature of the incident, and Andy at home alone when the light came to the house. But then Rooster dropped a bombshell. He said that Andy felt during the event that "purple people were trying to abduct him," and that while he didn't see any alien beings, "he could hear their voices."

"What did they say to him?" I asked.

"He couldn't understand them. It was gobbledygook. He didn't know what they were saying."

Why hadn't Andy mentioned these important details to me? Because I hadn't asked. Not wanting to "lead the witness," I had avoided asking him about contact or communication.

Rooster clarified that when the event began, Andy put the dog out in the yard and "it was freaking out." He thinks the dog's name was Cathy.

I asked if Rooster and his wife saw anything when they arrived home that evening.

"No, we didn't see any lights, nothing. But Andy told us all about it. Around that same time, Hughes (DB: a pseudonym for a close friend of Rooster's at the time), told us that he was coming home late from work one night and saw a UFO passing back and forth over a field near our house. Maybe that was the same UFO that shined down a light on Andy."

Rooster also reminded me of a UFO sighting that Andy had about two years ago, which I had heard about from Andy himself when it happened. Andy, who now lives in Portland, Oregon, with his family, saw an orange light in the night sky over the downtown Portland area. This was on the Fourth of July. Andy's oldest son, Mark (a pseudonym), had been saying all day long, "I want to see a UFO, I want to see a UFO," and then that night, the family did see one. Rooster says it's as if the boy had summoned the UFO and that there was a similar sighting of an orange

UFO in Seattle, Washington, on that same day. Andy captured a video of the orange orb on his cellphone, which I've seen.

Rooster's daughter, Tammy (Andy's sister), also had a UFO sighting sometime in the 1970s or '80s. She was with a girlfriend driving on 9th Street in Corvallis, Oregon, when they saw a giant UFO that was traveling north, in the direction of Salem.

Beth's Reptilian Visitor

Earl Heriot is the father of four daughters, all of whom have had a variety of paranormal experiences that were not obviously related to aliens or UFOs, such as poltergeist activity, and seeing or feeling the presence of paranormal entities. Only two of his daughters have seen UFOs, and just one of those has had experiences with what she believed may have been alien beings.

Earl's daughter, Beth, has had more alien and UFO-related experiences than her older sister, Sheila, who has had only two UFO sightings. In 2003, when Beth was pregnant with the first of her two sons, she had a frightening nighttime visitation from a threatening Reptilian-type humanoid alien. She and the father of her unborn child, Willy, were asleep in a friend's apartment where they were staying in Salem, Oregon, when Beth was startled awake by an intense feeling that a stranger was in the room very nearby. What she saw when she opened her eyes completely terrified Beth. There was a strange creature standing behind the head of the bed, between the bed and the wall, hanging over her, that looked like a cross between a man and a lizard. It was tall, covered in scales, and gave off a powerful sense of hostility. Although the intruder did not speak out loud, she clearly sensed that it wanted to take the fetus from her womb. Beth's entire being rebelled at the horror of this and she tried to screamed out "No!!!!" Her mouth was open and she felt like she was screaming, but no sound was coming out. She wasn't really sure if she was screaming vocally; perhaps she was just screaming it in her mind. Willy had no awareness that this scene was happening a few feet away, and remained deep asleep throughout the entire incident. After she rejected the idea of surrendering her baby to this monstrosity, the creature shifted its attention to her partner who was sleeping on his back to her left. The creature hung over him, and Beth got the distinct impression that it was about to attack him physically, at which point she again tried to scream, this time demanding that it "Go away!" She doesn't know if she was actually able to say the words out loud or if she only directed them at the creature mentally. The ominous being then left and Beth instantly fell back to sleep.

The next day, she vividly recalled this nightmarish event and excitedly told Earl and me about it. Although I didn't make any notes at the time, I clearly recall what she told me.

Oddly, Beth herself currently only remembers the second half of the event, when she saw the creature hanging over Willy. She doesn't remember the part about it wanting her baby. "It was in a very predatory position," she says, "like a cat stalking something. It got close to his face. I was seeing it, and trying to scream, but I couldn't make any noise. Then I thought I woke up again, although I already

Beth Heriot's sketch of the Reptilian alien that loomed over her as she slept one night in 2003. She sensed that the creature wanted to take the unborn baby she was carrying. *Computer sketch by Beth Heriot, 2016.*

felt very awake, and everything was normal. The experience with the creature was like a dream within a dream, yet it all seemed real, unlike any dream. I felt like I was fully awake throughout the whole thing." She speculates that possibly the experience was a case of "sleep paralysis—some terrible nightmare thing."

I asked Beth if she recalls any details of the being's appearance. "I remember he seemed tall, but with how he was hanging over Willy it was hard to tell exactly how tall. Seemed bigger than Willy, and Willy is 6'3" and 260 lbs. It was pretty dark, but I remember dark, greenish skin tones and scaly skin. I think he was wearing something like a vest kind of thing maybe, but I can't remember too well." Then I asked if the being spoke or made any sounds. "I only remember some kind of hissing sound while I was trying to scream. It seemed to be coming from him. He looked like he was trying to suck Willy's soul out of his throat or something. I'll try to sketch a little picture of the position of his body." (See Beth's drawing above.) Beth says about her drawing, "I didn't do the hands very well at all. The hands were big and had long pointy claw-like fingers."

My questions piqued her curiosity and Beth Googled "Reptilian aliens" and found the website www.bibliotecapleyades.net/vida_alien/alien_races00.htm. On the site, "TAL LeVesque" (Jason Bishop) described Reptilians as being large ("built like Bigfoot"), with large scales on the chest and smaller scales in flexible areas of the body. The green to dark green scales are similar to those on a snake. They have three fingers and an opposable thumb on each hand, and claws on both hands and feet. They have a small tail. The beings wear no clothes but have utility belts that hold unusual objects. They are highly telepathic and react to human thoughts.

Although Beth thought the website bizarre, she had to admit the description of a Reptilian closely matched what she had seen. "Funny how it sounds very similar. The way they describe the scales were like what I saw. I thought he wore a vest sort of thing but I wasn't sure. There was some kind of gear. Maybe belts, like the website says. And as the site says, the creature was built very large."

Never Forget the Pinecone Triangles

Beth says that before the experience with the Reptilian, when she was pregnant and staying at the home of a couple for whom she provided child daycare, Willy bought a bunch of alien abduction books by Whitley Strieber. "He got the books and then suddenly I couldn't sleep anymore. I woke up every night at exactly 3:33 a.m., the same time every damned night, and it started when he got those books."

And before that, she says, before she became pregnant, there was a strange thing that happened the first time Willy bought a UFO book. They were staying at his sister's house in North Salem, and Beth was working at a bookshop in West Salem. Early every morning he would take the bus with her from his sister's house to the street the bookstore was on. They would sit on the bench at a bus stop waiting for the store to open and her shift to begin, and every morning they noticed a bizarre construction on the ground beside the bench: a large triangle made of pinecones, several feet wide, the cones forming perfectly straight lines for the three edges of the triangle. Every morning they would mess up the construction, scatter the pinecones, and the next morning it would always be there again. The bench was in an isolated spot, with very few people around. She thought the triangle formation might have something to do with Willy's UFO book and she wrote about this connection but later could not find her writings. All she can remember is a single line from what she wrote: "Never forget the pinecone triangles!" Beth says it's as if just having UFO books around made strange things happen in her life.

Weird Handprints

After her first son was born, Beth—always a night owl—often would step out onto the balcony of their upstairs apartment in the middle of the night for a cigarette while the baby slept. On several occasions, late at night or in the early hours of the morning, she saw mysterious lights cavorting about the black skies—lights that did not look like or move like conventional aircraft or natural celestial objects. Willy, who worked nights, missed most of these sightings. She would always tell me and Earl about them, knowing of our interest in UFOs. She never formed a solid opinion as to what these lights might be; all she knew for certain was that they couldn't be explained away as commonplace airplanes, stars, planets, or meteors. Always interested in science, Beth knew enough about astronomy to know that she wasn't mistaking the Moon or Venus for a spaceship from another world.

When her son was a year old, in 2004, Beth awoke one morning to find "weird handprints" on the outside surface of one of the windows of their apartment. As before, she told Earl and me about this incident shortly after it occurred. At that time, Beth said the prints looked like they were "smeared with some sort of clear jelly" on the glass, and that the image of "the palm of a hand, with long fingers" was clearly visible in several of the greasy smears. What she could not fathom was how the prints had gotten where they were, because the apartment was on the second or third floor, which was high enough that the impressions couldn't have been made easily from the ground level. This particular window was not near a balcony or other structure that would have allowed a prankster to get close enough to the window to make such prints. It truly was a mystery to her. I wish she had photographed the prints, but this was before Beth had a cellphone with a built-in camera, and while she did own a 35mm camera, she didn't have any film for it at the time.

Orange Orbs

Over the years, Beth has continued to see strange lights in the sky. One evening after dinner in February 2016, she went out on her apartment balcony to have a smoke and noticed three brightly pulsating orange-red orbs moving around oddly in the sky behind some tall trees near her apartment in King City, Oregon, where she lives with her husband, Jerry Baron (a pseudonym, not to be confused with Earl's younger brother, Jerry Heriot. Beth broke up with Willy after their second son was born.). She called Jerry and her sons out to see the odd lights. This multiple-witness sighting lasted about five minutes, most of which she captured on video using her phone. You can hear the comments of Beth and her family in the video as they describe the appearance and movement of the objects, as well as their speculation that they are watching true UFOs and not conventional aircraft or heavenly bodies. Beth submitted a written report on the sighting to MUFON, along with her video, which supports her testimony.

Beth describes the completely silent objects as moving extremely quickly at times, making sudden changes in direction, hovering other times, and their shapes morphing now and then. The orange-red light they gave off was extremely bright, and she couldn't make out any structured craft behind it. Beth says the objects "looked like they were made of fire, but not burning in a fire way. Almost like a glowing coal." The quality of the light was not well captured in the video, although the objects are clearly visible. Rather than flying off into the distance at the end of the sighting, the objects simply disappeared into thin air. She says that in their movements, the objects "didn't seem to be following the general laws of gravity or propulsion."

Saucer Over the Observatory

Another of Earl Heriot's daughters, Sheila, remembers seeing a UFO when she was a child in 1980. At that time, Earl and his wife, Jane, were living in Southern California with their two young daughters: Sheila, who was five years old, and

Kelly, who was seven. Beth, Earl's third daughter, and Amy, the fourth and youngest of the four sisters, had not yet been born. One weekend, the family visited Griffith Observatory, perched high on the side of Mount Hollywood in Los Angeles. It was a sunny day and they were outside the Observatory building. Their parents were off someplace nearby, and Sheila and Kelly were playing in an open grassy area, rolling down a hill. "I looked up and saw a big classic flying saucer thing directly above," claims Sheila. Then she recalls saying, "Kelly, look at that! Do you see that?" She says the image of it is crystal clear, like a movie playing in her mind, but she's never been sure if it was real or imagined or a dream. The entire memory is very short—a matter of seconds.

If the memory is of an actual event, only the two girls saw it. Earl and his wife were not aware of what the children were seeing. When I asked Kelly about it in September 2016, she told me she recalls the two of them "talking about seeing a UFO" at the Observatory, but she believes the incident may have been imaginary—a case of wishful thinking on the part of two impressionable little girls who knew of their father's interest in the subject and wanted to please him with a good story. Given both sisters' doubts about the physical reality of the sighting, this story has to be taken with a grain of salt. It may not be a real sighting, although it is still interesting, given Earl Heriot's long history of UFO sightings and close encounters with aliens.

I pressed Sheila for more details about the UFO. She says it was hovering much lower than an airplane flying at standard cruising elevation—about one-fourth that height. The disk was large—as wide as a house or larger. It was silver in color, like the classic 1950s flying saucers, and it had a dome on top. She had no sense of contact or communication with the craft or its occupants during or after the event. She doesn't recall if it flew off or simply disappeared at the end of the sighting.

A String of Christmas Tree Lights

Sheila's second UFO sighting happened many years later, when she was an adult, and involved multiple witnesses. I have no doubt that it was an actual unexplained event. The year was 1996, or 1997, and she was twenty or twenty-one years old and living in Port Townsend, Washington. On a warm summer evening, she and two friends visited another friend in what she calls "a small hippie village" in the woods near Chimacum, Washington, which is about ten miles south of Port Townsend on the Olympic Peninsula. The village consisted of five or six trailers parked in the woods, occupied by young people, some of whom she knew. The friend they were visiting had a trailer there and the village was having a "block party." It was early evening and still light out when they arrived around six or seven o'clock p.m. They parked the car on some flat land and walked up a hill to the trailers, which were scattered through the woods, a short distance apart. Sheila hadn't had anything to drink and didn't use drugs; she was completely sober.

When they reached the first trailer, Sheila was startled to see lights buzzing all around the area.

> The orbs were everywhere, flying through the trees. They were pastel colors, muted shades of pink, yellow, green, and blue. They followed one another in long lines, spaced apart about the same as bulbs on a string of Christmas tree lights, and they were about the same size as Christmas tree lights. They were very active, dancing, swirling, spinning, and zooming around playfully, like fairies or fireflies.

She saw them clearly, but none of her friends did. She asked each person she encountered, "Do you see that, the lights?" but no one did or at least they didn't admit to it.

> The orbs were not at all scary or creepy or threatening. They were really fascinating and beautiful, but I was frustrated because I wanted verification of what I was seeing, and I wanted it explained to me. They were everywhere we went, from trailer to trailer, and very dense. After a while, we grabbed a beer but I limited myself to just that one because I wanted to keep my wits about me so that I could be sure of what I was seeing. All evening, I casually asked people if they saw the orbs, and they all said no. This went on for a couple of hours and the lights were pretty constant.

Still frustrated, she left the party and wandered deeper into the woods, looking for someone else who might have seen the lights. The orbs continued to swirl around her but she was not afraid. A couple of trailers down—about a five-minute walk—she met some hippie kids and introduced herself. Once she got talking with them, they brought up the subject of the orbs, asking her if she saw them, too. "Aren't they cool?" asked one of the hippies.

Sheila was greatly relieved that somebody else besides her could see the weird lights. They described the orbs to her, and their description exactly matched what she was seeing. She was careful not to ask them any leading questions, nor to give them any information about what she saw, so that she could trust the detailed description they gave her. After a while, she returned to her friends, and they left. The entire experience lasted about three hours.

I asked Sheila if she had ever seen anything else like these orbs. She said she has seen small white lights similar to the orbs at Chimacum while walking in natural areas but each time it was only a single white light, which was usually what she called "a warm white." Chimacum is the only place she's seen colored orbs, and there they were "heavy and constant" as opposed to a solitary orb. She guesses she saw hundreds of them that night. She asked so many people about them at the party that after a while she stopped asking. "I was starting to feel nuts," she says. "The verification from the hippie kids was all the proof I needed that these orbs were really there, and that I was not imagining them. I have zero doubts about it. It's a sure thing."

Sheila told me she was doing a lot of Yoga meditation to relax at the time of the Chimacum sighting, and that her mind was "open to the experience, with no mental barriers to it." That might be why she could see what others couldn't.

The duration of this sighting, plus the large number of objects seen, and the verification by multiple witnesses, make this a highly unusual incident. Was it a true UFO sighting, in other words, a phenomenon somehow related to alien activity, or was it paranormal in nature? That's hard to say, although many people have speculated that there is some connection between light orbs and aliens.

Connect the Dots

Yet another member of Earl Heriot's family who has seen UFOs is his son-in-law, Jerry Baron (Beth's husband). Long before the couple met, when he was about fourteen years old, Jerry had a dramatic UFO sighting that involved several disk-shaped objects observed over a period of about an hour by a total of four witnesses. He thinks the year was probably 1994. This occurred on the Hood Canal in Washington State's Puget Sound. The canal is located about thirty miles west of Seattle. Jerry's grandfather had a cabin on the canal and every summer over the Fourth of July holiday his family stayed there. That particular summer, his parents, some of their adult friends, Jerry, his brother, the brother's girlfriend, and a friend of Jerry's were at the cabin. The four teenagers went outside as it was beginning to get dark around 9:00 p.m. on the night of July 5. At that time, the sky was mostly clear. The four of them sat out on the back porch, which was right on the canal, and talked while the adults stayed inside. Jerry's brother was the first one to spot the seven UFOs hovering in the sky over the canal. He pointed them out to the other teenagers and together they watched the objects. Jerry says the objects were not too far away and he could see them clearly. They were stationary in the sky—not moving at all.

After about a half-hour, a cloud cover came in and a lightning storm started rather suddenly. As soon as the storm began, the objects started moving around. Jerry says they moved just like hummingbirds: darting very quickly, stopping very abruptly, and their movements were extremely precise. All of the UFOs moved like that but one at a time. A UFO would suddenly move, stop, then another moved and it stopped, and so on, with each one "hitting its mark, but not in a straight line." Once all seven UFOs were in position, "lightning would strike through all seven of them, like it was playing connect the dots." After the strike, they would all move again into a new configuration and the lightning would strike again.

This display went on for some time, during which the kids went inside to get the binoculars. They told his parents what they were seeing outside but none of the adults seemed to believe them, and none of them cared anyway. His parents were Mormons and UFOs didn't fit into their belief system.

The teenagers took the binoculars outside and used them to get a better look at the UFOs. According to Jerry, "They were saucer-shaped. The top was dark black. The bottom was a pearly silver, like mother-of-pearl. There was a clearly defined rim to the saucer." The very quick movements convinced him that the objects were not man-made. Nor were they any sort of natural phenomenon such as ball lightning. The objects' high speed, acceleration, sudden stops, and precise movements between lightning strikes suggested to him an advanced technology.

What he calls "a game of connect the dots with the lightning" went on for a half-hour to forty-five minutes, at which point the four witnesses lost track of the objects in the thickening cloud cover.

I asked Jerry if he could estimate the size and distance of the objects, but he couldn't as there was no frame of reference. He saw no details on the objects such as windows, doors, or other structural features. It was simply the black top, the rim, and the silvery bottom. I also asked if he thought the objects might have been over the surrounding hills or if they were closer, over the water. He is sure they were over the canal itself, which is roughly two miles wide where the cabin is located.

"Did you have any sense of contact or communication with the objects or their occupants?" I asked.

"No. All I felt was a sense of wonderment. I'd always wondered if UFOs existed, but I didn't put that much thought into it. I didn't believe in them, but I didn't rule them out, either. After that sighting, it was undeniable that there was something real to the subject. I'm sure what we saw were artificial craft, and nothing natural. All four of us saw these things."

"Had you read much about UFOs before this?"

"No."

I asked if he had any guesses about what might have been happening during the event. "What impressed me was the immense power of the lightning strikes. If you're looking to recharge your batteries, that's going to do it."

"Any further thoughts?" I asked.

"Yes. The storm seemed odd. It was a clear night for the most part, and the storm came up suddenly. I wondered if they—the UFOs—caused it, or if they knew it would come and were waiting for it."

Non-Participants

Not everyone in Earl Heriot's family has seen UFOs or had suspected encounters with aliens. His younger brother, Jerry Heriot, has never had a UFO sighting. Likewise, Earl's wife, Jane, doesn't have a history of paranormal experiences or unexplained sightings, although she and their daughters, Kelly and Sheila, did see the so-called "Long Beach Blimp UFO" when he pointed it out to them from the parking lot of a Von's Shopping Center in 1982. But Jane currently has no memory of that event, although she believes Earl when he tells her that she said she saw it at the time. Like their mother, neither Kelly nor Sheila recall this sighting. Could this mean that Earl is mistaken and that Jane, Kelly, and Sheila did not observe this object—in effect that he is incorrectly remembering the event? Or does it mean that while the three of them did see it at the time, for some reason they do not retain conscious memory of it at the present?

Earl's youngest daughter, Amy, has had ghost sightings and other weird experiences, but no UFO sightings. "They scare me and I block it from my mind. I don't allow myself to even think about the subject," she told me. It occurred to me that she could be having UFO-related experiences and is not allowing herself to remember them, but why needlessly disturb her peace of mind by suggesting this to her? Life is difficult enough without looking for things to worry about.

CHAPTER 7

CHAPTER 7
I, Hybrid

(by Jordan)

> What I'm doing will either be an interesting but non-essential footnote to popular culture or the most important thing that's ever happened to humankind. I see it as the latter.
>
> —Dr. David M. Jacobs
>
> International Center for Abduction Research

Am I a hybrid? Do I carry implanted alien nucleic acid sequences in my genome? It's possible. I have always been alienated by this culture. Many of my geopolitical opinions are from an extraterrestrial perspective. I am also a "limited precog." But if I am a hybrid I must not be very promising to the alien gene tinkerers, whatever their ultimate purpose for hybridizing our species with theirs. Of course none of this counts for a 2,000-piece-puzzle of the bright blue sky. It is possible I am a hybrid but not probable. I do, however, know people very close to me who might be hybrids. But more on that later.

Two recent books have dramatically attempted to answer the hybrid question: David M. Jacobs' *Walking Among Us: The Alien Plan to Control Humanity* and Nick Redfern's *Bloodline of the Gods.* Both books approach the hybrid issue from different intriguing angles. Jacobs argues for the relatively recent emergence of hybrids and Redfern suggests that hybrids have been around since Homo erectus (1.8 million to about 50,000 years ago).

Jacobs' intriguing take on the subject is that hybridization has taken decades or centuries and began with the insectalin aliens (or "mantids") hybridizing with humans (Jacobs 20–21), resulting in small Grays (Ibid. 21). "Small Grays are basically helpers" (Ibid. 28). Their roles include abducting people from their homes, assisting in procedures aboard craft, and bringing the abductees home after the examination. This fits with the view of Grays as biological drones, the "worker bees" of alien hives.

Small Grays were further hybridized into tall Grays (Ibid. 21–22) that "perform more complex procedures on abductees—egg-and-sperm harvesting, embryo implantation, fetal extraction, and neurological engagement" (Ibid. 29). These are the Grays with which abductees have most of their interactions aboard craft. They seem more intelligent and self-sufficient than the small Grays, who are often witnessed assisting the tall Grays in medical procedures, etc.

Tall Grays were hybridized into early-stage humanoid hybrids with a thin body; wispy hair; diminished nose, mouth, and ears; human eyes with only a little white showing; pointed chin; sexual organs typical of human male and female; telepathy; and energy and nutrients absorbed through the skin. "Their primary activity is to take care of hybrid babies and toddlers" (Ibid. 30).

Early-stage humanoid hybrids were hybridized into middle-stage humanoid hybrids with a half-alien, half-human face, thicker hair, small nose and mouth, pointed chin, more human-looking eyes, male and female sexes, and telepathy (Ibid. 23–24). They also are tasked with taking care of hybrid toddlers as well as older children, and "sometimes perform procedures on humans" (Ibid. 30). From abductee accounts of this stage, sexual intercourse is often initiated by humanoid hybrids. They seem to be learning about human sexuality from the abductees, even if that sexuality is rape by any name. Some male hybrids are overly sexually aggressive or just simply do not know what to do with the parts; it is the abductee who instructs the hybrid on how to have sex with a human being.

Middle-stage humanoid hybrids led to late-stage humanoid hybrids, often lacking body hair but with head hair present, appearance pretty much identical to human beings, human reproduction and waste removal systems present, both male and female sexes, food eaten with mouth, and mostly telepathic but capable of speech (Ibid. 24). Late-stage male humanoid hybrids often bond with human females and have repeated sexual intercourse with them over decades (Ibid. 30–31).

Human-stage hybrids are next, designed to be "advance and security hybrids" that are completely indistinguishable from humans, with a function-oriented mentality; males are "security hybrids," and both sexes comprise the "advance hybrids" that eat with the mouth and are capable of telepathy and speech (Ibid. 24–25). Their function is "to ensure that the hubrids [hybridized human-stage hybrids] who are living on Earth are adjusting smoothly" as well as "finding housing" for the hubrids and as "security hybrids" who "keep abductees quiet," as ominous as that sounds (Ibid. 31). These hybrids may very well comprise the Men In Black and family (more on this later).

The final step in all this hybridization is the "hubrid." Hubrids are almost exactly the same as humans but capable of telepathy. Hubrids are the invaders into our society and will, Jacobs proposes, replace us humans one day completely, just as modern *Homo sapiens* replaced Neandertals through competition for resources and interbreeding (Ibid. 25, 31–32). This new species of hubrids and hubrid-human hybrids are called *Homo alienus* and they are our species' future incarnation.

Hubrids begin their education of human societies aboard ship in a kind of "Hybrid High." Even so, when they are released onto Earth they are often profoundly naïve, unable to comprehend the use of a refrigerator, for example. There are now "independent hubrids" and "group hubrids" living on Earth (Ibid. 32). Group hubrids often live together in the same housing arrangement, relying on each other and an abductee attendant to assist them. Independent hubrids rely on abductees for instruction to integration in human society: finding an apartment, a job, necessities at shops, how to put food in a fridge, and so on.

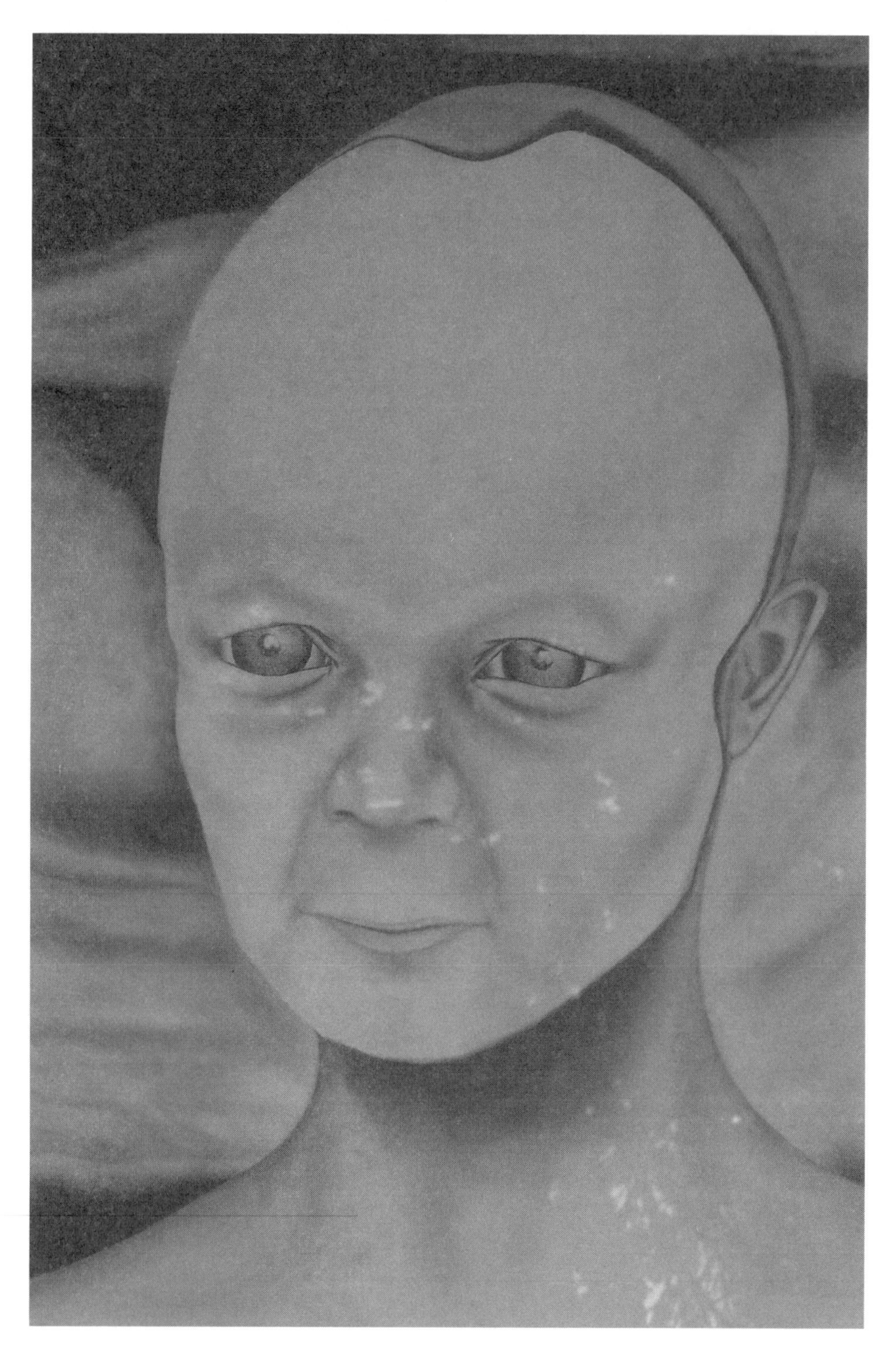

"Hubrid Experiment." *Homo alienus* or an earlier stage in hybridization? *Graphite on paper, 22" x 30", by Chris Olsenius, 1996. Photograph by Jordan Hofer, 2016.*

Abductees refer to this late-stage hubrid program as the "Change" (Ibid. 39). It is, if Jacobs is correct, a change that will lead our unhybridized species to extinction. Hardly an optimistic prospect but not at all unheard of in human evolution. More than twenty species of human have gone extinct in the last six million years, leaving us the sole human inheritors of the planet. If the hubrids are more successful than any given human, reproductively speaking, then we could be replaced. When modern *Homo sapiens* replaced the Neandertals they did so rather quickly, geologically speaking, in about 15,000 years; this was accomplished, primarily, by the 0.1 percent difference in reproduction rate between the two species. If the hubrids can top 0.1 percent over us they may very well be contenders for rule of the planet.

Jacobs comments, "The evidence I have found points in one direction, and that is the integration of hubrids into human society for an eventual take-over. I have found no evidence to refute this" (Ibid. 46).

But I must pause and consider this insidious domination. If hubrids are truly indistinguishable from humans, then how on Earth will they survive the massive breakdown of the biosphere that is currently accelerating towards a disastrous end including, most probably, nuclear annihilation? So what kind of world are these hubrids and their gray and insectalin progenitors willing to live in? The oceans will be dead expanses of acidic seas. Radiation will ravage the living. Freshwater will be unobtainable unless a very sophisticated means of desalinization and detoxification can be achieved. What will they eat? After being trained to function in human society, what will the hubrids do when that society is utterly obliterated? The aliens know very well the situation our planet is in, as they screen apocalyptic images to terrified abductees. Do they have a plan for the virtual end of life on Earth? From the ufology literature, it does not appear that the aliens give a damn for the environment. So where does this leave the hubrids? Perhaps they will adapt at the individual level to the toxic planet. Who knows? My point is that the aliens are going through a lot of toil to inherit a virtually dead planet. Maybe they have some kind of "Genesis Device" that will revitalize the ailing biosphere; that, at least, is some kind of hope for this doomsday scenario.

Nick Redfern addresses Jacobs' book in *Women In Black* (2016):

> In 2015, Dr. David M. Jacobs' book, *Walking Among Us: The Alien Plan to Control Humanity*, was published . . . Although it is heavily focused on so-called "alien abductees," it is not actually about abduction events at all. Rather, its focus is on how abductees are allegedly being used to assist alien-human hybrids whose role it is to infiltrate human society. And, yes, that word "infiltrate" is intended to suggest that nothing good can come from any of it . . . the invasion, take-over, and/or extermination, will be completed before we'll have a single chance to do anything about it (Redfern 2016: 64).

Redfern too is talking about hybrids in his book *Bloodline of the Gods* (2015), only his speculation states that hybridization took place hundreds of thousands of years ago, which he attributes to the Annunaki gene tampering with *Homo erectus*. The resulting hybrids are identifiable today by Rh negative blood type.

Before digging into the thesis of Redfern's book, I would be remiss not to address a couple points that are just plain incorrect. I do this as a student (and former teacher) of human evolution, not to point out any personal fault of Redfern. We're human and we make errors.

Redfern says that the very existence of Rh negatives goes "against everything that Charles Darwin stood for, and that Darwinism and the Theory of Evolution still stand for, today" (Redfern 2015:11). Actually, no living form contradicts Darwin's theory. In fact, evolution by means of natural selection is the only theory that can explain anything biological, even the domesticates and genetic chimeras. The Rh negatives can usually only produce a second offspring with other Rh negatives, and Redfern assumes this to mean that selection could not possibly produce such an insular mating group. Since Rh negative women cannot ordinarily carry a second Rh positive child (this results in hemolytic disease in the newborn, as the woman's blood through the umbilical reacts to the neonate as it would to foreign tissue), Redfern assumes this variation would have gone extinct if not for alien intervention. But this just is not so. Rh negatives are not entirely insular. They can conceive a first child with an Rh positive individual, but without proper drug treatments the next child will die of hemolytic disease. And there is also the matter of population maintenance via genetic drift.

The scientific paper "Evolutionary genetics of the human Rh blood group system" (Perry, et al 2012) suggests an evolutionary explanation for the maintenance of the Rh negative blood group in specific human populations:

> The evolutionary history of variation in the human Rh blood group system . . . has long been an unresolved puzzle in human genetics . . . [W]e used new molecular and genomic data . . . to test the idea that positive selection for an as-of-yet unknown fitness benefit . . . may have offset the otherwise negative fitness effects of hemolytic disease of the newborn . . . Thus, the initial rise to intermediate frequency . . . in European populations may simply be explained by genetic drift/founder effect . . . Therefore, once such a frequency was achieved, it could have been maintained by a relatively small amount of genetic drift.

In other words, the form of the gene responsible for hemolytic disease is selected again by the maintenance of the gene coding for Rh negative; therefore, selection will favor the Rh negative gene in a population much in the same way that sickle cell anemia is maintained by the heterozygote's resistance to malaria. This does not go against evolution at all. This is evolution.

Another error concerning human evolution is found on page forty-four of Redfern's controversial book: ". . . [T]he Neandertals . . . almost certainly built boats and sailed the seas . . . [and] were seasoned farmers . . ." In all the years I've studied and taught human evolution, I've never heard, even as a speculation, that the Neandertals "built boats and sailed the seas." There is zero evidence for this claim. The Neandertals' range was from Asia, through the Middle East, and into Europe. No evidence has ever been found that supports the contention that Neandertals sailed boats. A possibility exists that *Homo erectus* built and sailed watercraft, but even this is contentious, as the species probably made their way to islands in Indonesia

The Lesson of Ardipithecus. An android instructs hybrids about human evolution. *Oil on canvas, 48" x 36", by Chris Olsenius, 2015. Photograph by Jordan Hofer, 2016.*

via natural rafting (i.e., a massive storm would sweep the hominins along with trees and other floating wrack until landfall on an island or other distant landmass). Another error is that Neandertals "were seasoned farmers." They were not. Neandertals were hunter-gatherers. They hunted big game and gathered fruits, vegetables, and tubers. The last Neandertal individual lived about 35,000 years ago. Agriculture was not innovated until around 12,000 years ago, and it was achieved by fully modern *Homo sapiens*, first in Mesopotamia and then rapidly all over the planet.

Redfern notes five populations in which the Rh negative variation is high in frequency: Brazilians, Basques, Celts, Gaels, and Welsh (Ibid. 112, 130, 189). These are the descendants of the "gods," according to Redfern, as well as anyone else who is Rh negative, the direct result of gene tampering hundreds of thousands of years ago. Without the mechanisms of evolution, this conclusion does not make much sense. Something had to be selecting positively for the gene that results in Rh negative blood, and genetic drift explains this. Still, Redfern's hypothesis of Rh negatives as the result of alien hybridization is intriguing.

Ordinarily, identifying specific groups and individuals as "the Other," has led to unfortunate demonizing and violent reprisal against these "Others." At first, this bothered me about Redfern's book. He certainly views human variation typologically. But I realized that no one (the government and other powers capable of targeting a specific group en masse) outside the ufology community would even consider Redfern's speculations. Therefore, I believe that the backlash against Rh negatives and other suspected hybrids will never occur. No discrimination against any group has turned out well for society, especially for those members whom the current society perceives as the dangerous "Other."

Redfern even "outs" some individuals with Rh negative blood including Betty Andreasson, George H. W. Bush, Bill Clinton, Queen Elizabeth II and Prince Charles, Dwight D. Eisenhower, (possibly) Barney and Betty Hill, John F. Kennedy, Richard Nixon, Lee Harvey Oswald (and his Russian wife), Brad Steiger, and Erich von Danniken (Ibid. 143, 189, 205–207, 218, 219).

In response to being outed as a hybrid, Brad Steiger had this to say in a personal email correspondence:

> Well, I don't know about the alien hybrid aspect, but I do have the Rh negative blood and the majority of the traits you list [further in this chapter]. My mother used to tease that they found me out in a field at the end of a plowed-up pile of soil. But I have seen pictures of her pregnant with me, so I know she was teasing. She was also Danish and loved to laugh.

Redfern describes the common hybrid as it became known to abductees in the 1990s: "They looked human, but there were certain things that were just not right. Their skin was pale, almost to the point of appearing anemic. Their limbs were thin, bony, and fragile-looking. Their eyes were overly large, and noticeably oval- or almond-shaped, exactly like those of the Grays" (Ibid. 156).

A strange addition to the hybrid pantheon are the "Black-Eyed Children," or what I call the "Kids In Black" (KIB). Are these the offspring of the Men In Black and their counterparts, the Women In Black, perhaps a "Family In Black"? Their "familial" equation would then be MIB + WIB + KIB = FIB. I leave the irony with no punchline here.

Redfern describes the Black-Eyed Children as "acutely skinny and pale in the extreme" (Ibid. 169) wearing black clothing, often "a black hoodie" (Ibid.); their "entire eye is black" (Ibid.). Redfern states that the Black-Eyed Children "are just the latest, unearthly addition to the alien bloodline" (Ibid.).

The Black-Eyed Children surveil abductees with planned encounters. They have the "ability to near-hypnotize people" (Ibid. 170), and can disappear instantly, both of which are capabilities of the Grays.

I gave the two questionnaires below to probable suspected abductees and to possible hybrids, Mike and Jackie Montgomery, my friends and witnesses of the "Salem Low-Flying Triangle" case. In previous interviews with the Montgomery family, Mike had claimed to see aliens, Jackie was terrified of considering hypnotic regression, and their daughter had suspected interactions, if not abductions, with aliens. I fully expected to discover confirmation of the Montgomerys' abductions and maybe even alien hybrid traits.

Before determining whether or not someone is a hybrid, it is first helpful to screen them for abductee status using the "Experiencer Questionnaire" on MUFON's website, as designed and first administered by Kathleen Marden and Denise Stoner (www.mufon.com/experiencer-questionnaire.html):

1) Have you had a close encounter with a UFO?

Mike: Yes. One confirmed. An equilateral black triangle with strobing white lights that produced a deep thrumming noise.
Jackie: Yes. Two. The first when I was a teenager. My sister and I saw a large craft in the shape of an isosceles triangle with red and green lights on the underside as well as a glowing blue rectangle. The second sighting was the same as Mike's. Our son was also a witness to that one.

2) Do you consciously recall (not with hypnosis), the observation of non-human entities immediately prior to an abduction while you were outside your home?

Mike: No.
Jackie: Nope.

3) Have witnesses observed a UFO near your house, vehicle, tent, etc., prior to or during your abduction?

Mike: To my knowledge, I have not been abducted.
Jackie: Nope.

4) Have you experienced at least an hour of missing time following a close encounter with a UFO for which you can find no prosaic explanation?

Mike: I have had an incident of missing time, but not associated with a UFO. Probably due to sleep deprivation.
Jackie: No.

5) Have you awoken in bed to find beings in your bedroom? Did you move your body or cry out and then become paralyzed?

Mike: Beings other than my children, no.
Jackie: I have had plenty of dreams of children in my bedroom.

6) Do you have memories of moving rapidly through the air under someone else's control when you were awake in bed and observed intruders in your bedroom?

Mike: No.
Jackie: No.

7) Do you consciously recall part of an abduction experience?

Mike: No.
Jackie: No.

8) Are you aware of having been examined on an alien craft?

Mike: No.
Jackie: No.

9) Have you had recurring dreams/ nightmares about alien abduction?

Mike: Not of an abduction but a UFO. I have a recurring dream about a UFO sighting at my grandmother's house. A robin's-egg-blue glowing, pulsing cigar-shaped UFO comes over the top of my grandparents' barn in winter in Wisconsin. I wake up in terror.
Jackie: No.

10) Do you occasionally hear strange code-like buzzing sounds in your ears similar to tinnitus, or hear telepathic messages, or feel a strange but familiar sensation that you'll have an abduction experience that night?

Mike: The code thing is interesting. Sometimes I hear strange buzzing noises.
Jackie: No.

11) Have you awoken feeling fearful and unwell, with memories of intruders in your home?

Mike: I have woken up feeling like there were probably aliens in my house and was afraid to get out of bed. But I have never been afraid since we moved to our new house.
Jackie: No.

12) Have you awoken with unexplained marks on your body, such as cored out areas of tissue, triangle-shaped burns, finger-shaped bruises, or a sunburn without exposure to the sun?

Mike: Yes. I have lines of broken blood vessels on the top of my shoulders. It looks like I've been whipped but with no welts. The blood vessels under the skin have burst.
Jackie: No.

13) Have you awoken and found yourself dressed in someone else's clothing or with your own clothing inside out or backwards, without a prosaic explanation?

Mike: Five or six years ago I woke up totally buck naked and have no idea how that happened.
Jackie: No.

14) If you are a female, have you experienced a gynecological problem that you think is related to your abduction/contact experiences?

Jackie: No.

15) As a child, were you generally happy and without unusual highs and lows?

Mike: I had a reasonably happy childhood. I don't remember being a tortured youngster.
Jackie: Yes, I was happy as a child until middle school.

16) As an adult, are you generally happy and without unusual highs and lows?

Mike: I have my highs and lows but I'm pretty happy in general.
Jackie: Definitely.

17) Can you feel a foreign object in your body that you suspect is an alien implant?

Mike: Not that I suspect is an alien implant. Probably a tumor.
Jackie: No.

18) Have you awoken with memories of alien abduction and found that you are more sensitive to light?

Mike: I don't like light in general. But no.
Jackie: No.

19) Do you have difficulty falling asleep and remaining asleep due to fear of alien abduction?

Mike: Maybe difficulty falling asleep if I'm really drunk.
Jackie: Some trouble remaining asleep.

20) Have you been diagnosed as having Chronic Fatigue and Immune Dysfunction Syndrome or Reactivated Mononucleosis?

Mike: No, but I'm tired a lot.
Jackie: No.

21) Do you suffer from migraine headaches?

Mike: No.
Jackie: I used to, during my early twenties, mostly. Debilitating for a couple of years.

22) Have you awoken with burns, hair loss, or conjunctivitis and memories of an abduction/contact?

Mike: I have awoken with conjunctivitis but with no recollection of an alien encounter.
Jackie: No.

23) Has your nose bled immediately following a suspected abduction/contact?

Mike: No. But I do get nosebleeds from time to time.
Jackie: No.

24) Do you crave excessive amounts of salt?

Mike: Yes. I love salt.
Jackie: Definitely not.

25) Following a suspected abduction/contact, did you ever experience malfunctions of electrical equipment such as lights, digital watches, computers, appliances, all within a four-hour period?

Mike: I am constantly swearing at machines, but no.
Jackie: No.

26) Have you witnessed paranormal activity in your home, such as light orbs, objects flying through the air, pictures flying off walls, lights turning off and on, windows opening and closing, doors opening and closing, and toilets flushing on their own?

Mike: No.
Jackie: No.

27) Are you more or less sensitive, intuitive, or psychic than you were before you had a memory of alien abduction?

Mike: Do you make these questions up or do they just write them down for you?
Jackie: No.

28) Do you possess information about alien technology that you've never read or learned in your normal environment?

Mike: I wish, but no.
Jackie: No.

29) Have you had multiple sightings of UFOs up close?

Mike: No, just one.
Jackie: Two.

30) Do you have an inordinate fear of alien abduction that affects your everyday life?

Mike: I have a ridiculous fear of alien abduction that does not affect my everyday life.
Jackie: No.

If you answered 15 or more questions in the affirmative, you might be an ETI [Extraterrestrial Intelligence] contact experiencer.

The tally of positive answers provided by Mike adds up to nine, at its most liberal interpretation. Jackie's positive answers equal four. Some of their answers, however, are highly suggestive of some kind of alien contact, especially in light of earlier conversations. Both have witnessed UFOs up close. In answer to question four, Mike admits to missing time but attributes it to mere "sleep deprivation," not an encounter or abduction. Jackie replies to question five that she has had lots of dreams about children in her bedroom. These "children" could be interpreted as diminutive Grays. Mike replies to question nine that he does not awake from dreams of alien abduction per se but from a recurring dream of a UFO flying over his grandparents' barn in Wisconsin, a dream he has had since he was a child. Mike responds to question ten that he does sometimes hear strange buzzing noises, perhaps an aural message from extraterrestrial intelligences. To question eleven he fully admits to being aware of an alien presence at his former house but not, interestingly, at his new house. He witnessed the "Salem Low-Flying Triangle" from the porch of his former house. To question twelve he describes discovering burst blood vessels on his shoulders, beneath the skin. Did these lines of subdermal rupturing occur during an abduction? To thirteen he replies that he once awoke "buck naked" with absolutely no memory of how he got naked. Jackie answers question nineteen that she has some trouble staying asleep. This is probably due to her extremely industrious nature, but could suggest disturbances in dreams, perhaps of alien contact. She says in response to question twenty-one that she had "debilitating" migraine headaches in her early twenties, approximately ten years after her sighting of the isosceles craft with her sister. Mike has awakened with conjunctivitis but does not believe it has anything to do with abduction (question twenty-two). He also has nosebleeds "from time to time" (question twenty-three), again expressing no belief in a correlation with abduction. He loves salt (question twenty-four), but how that might correlate with abduction is unclear. Finally, in answer to question thirty, Mike admits to "a ridiculous fear of alien abduction," but nothing that adversely affects his daily life. Mike and Jackie tried to answer the questions as truthfully and seriously as possible but a lot of their responses are either humorous rejoinders or else flat-out rejection. Rejection that they might not have expressed if they were still living in their former house where Mike saw the triangular craft and his daughter played with "gnomes" in her bedroom at night. Still, the questions seem to reveal that Mike and Jackie are not abductees and never have been.

After abductee status is determined (positive or negative), the suspected hybrid can be identified by the following traits (1, 8, 17 and 18-30 provided by Brad Steiger in a personal email):

1) Rh negative blood type (or a combination of blood types).

Mike: No.
Jackie: Yes, I have O negative blood type. I had to take a lot of drugs to make sure I could have another child. My son is O negative and my daughter is positive.

2) Higher than average IQ (Ibid. 197).

Mike: That's what I'm told.
Jackie: Oh, yeah. That's why I've answered "no" to most of these questions.

3) Photosensitivity (Ibid. 198).

Mike: Yeah, I don't like light. I really hate the light—it's bright.
Jackie: No.

4) Blood pressure lower than 120/80 (Ibid. 199).

Mike: No, unfortunately.
Jackie: No.

5) Lower than normal body temperature (Ibid. 200).

Mike: No.
Jackie: Yes. I run about 97.1.

6) Lower than normal heart rate (Ibid.).

Mike: No.
Jackie: No, I don't think so.

7) Thoracic outlet syndrome (an extra rib) (Ibid.).

Mike: No.
Jackie: No.

8) Extra sixth lumbar (transitional vertebrae and fused vertebrae) (Ibid. 202).

Mike: No.
Jackie: No.

9) Extended cauda equina (a tail) (Ibid. 204).

Mike: No.
Jackie: Not myself, but my dad did. He had remnants that kept him out of the military.

10) Prophetic dreams (Ibid. 205).

Mike: No.
Jackie: No.

11) Synchronicities (Ibid.).

Mike: Only with my friend, Christian. I have an artistic psychic link with him.
Jackie: Nope.

12) ESP (Ibid.).

Mike: I didn't see that one coming.
Jackie: No, but I do have a good story. My dad had a high ESP rating when he was at university. He was really good at reading cards, etcetera. I think Dad may be a hybrid.

13) Mind-reading (Ibid.).

Mike: Nope.
Jackie: I'm really good at reading my children's minds.

14) Telepathy (Ibid.).

Mike: No.
Jackie: No, sadly, I don't.

15) Psychic bonds with animals (Ibid.).

Mike: [Laughter.]
Jackie: Nope.

16) Fascination with astronomy, outer space, extraterrestrials (Ibid.).

Mike: Ohhhhhhhhh, yes. It's certainly more essential than friendship on my Maslow's Hierarchy of Needs.
Jackie: It's all relative around here.

17) Feel [you] have been pre-programed for some task on Earth, waiting to be "switched on" (Ibid.) (Feel a great urgency, a short time to complete important goals, a special mission).

Mike: I want to believe. I do. But no.
Jackie: No.

18) Compelling eyes.

Mike: No.
Jackie: No.

19) Personal charisma.

Mike: My wife says I do. But I'm not like Face from *The A-Team*.
Jackie: No. [But Mike says she does.]

20) Hypersensitivity to electricity, electromagnetic fields.

Mike: No, I do not.
Jackie: No.

21) Chronic sinusitis.

Mike: Yes, oh my lord. It's horrible.
Jackie: No.

22) Thrive on little sleep and do [your] best work at night.

Mike: Yes.
Jackie: No.

23) [You were] an unexpected child.

Mike: No.
Jackie: No.

24) Sense that [your] true ancestors came from another world, another dimension, another level of consciousness, and yearn for [your] real home "beyond the stars."

Mike: No.
Jackie: No.

25) Experience a buzzing or a clicking sound or a high-pitched mechanical whine in the ears prior to, or during, some psychic event or warning of danger.

Mike: I don't believe so.
Jackie: No.

26) Had unseen companions as a child.

Mike: Nope.
Jackie: Yes. I had an imaginary little sister before my younger sister was born.

27) Had a dramatic experience around the age of five which often took the form of a white light and/or a visitation by human-appearing beings who gave information, guidance, or comfort.

Mike: No.
Jackie: Definitely not.

28) Have maintained a continuing contact with beings which [you] consider to be angels, masters, elves, spiritual teachers or openly declared UFO intelligences.

Mike: Other than my wife, no.
Jackie: No.

29) Had a serious accident, illness, traumatic experience or near-death experience around the age of eleven or twelve which encouraged [you] to turn inward.

Mike: No.
Jackie: No.

30) Have occupations helping and assisting the public.

Mike: Yes.
Jackie: Yes.

If you answered 15 or more questions in the affirmative, you might be an alien hybrid [following the scoring of the Marden-Stoner study].

Mike answered yes to only seven questions at most and Jackie eight. Jackie's blood type is Rh negative, as is her son's (question one). Her daughter's blood type is Rh positive and she is only alive because Jackie was given drug treatments during her first pregnancy to prevent hemolytic disease in future pregnancies. Both Mike and Jackie possess high IQs, as do both of their children (question two). I have known Mike for more than thirty-five years and have always known him to possess a keen intelligence, but nothing non-human. Likewise, I have known Jackie for more than twenty-seven years and have seen her intelligence and strength of will lead to success after success in her private and public lives. Mike is photosensitive—he hates bright light (question three). He loves to sleep. Jackie has a slightly lower than normal body temperature, but nothing outside the norm (question five). In answer to question nine, Jackie denies having a tail but her father had "remnants" of one. Most probably it was removed at birth and did not have any bone or muscle. Why any "remnant" would remain is odd, perhaps the result of an imperfect surgical removal. Mike has experienced synchronicities (question eleven) but only with his friend, Christian, which he attributes to a shared artistic vision. To question twelve, Jackie again mentions her father. Apparently he was a test subject in ESP experiments conducted by the government while he attended university. He could read the backs of cards and was pretty good at the tests administered. Jackie then suggests that her father might be a hybrid. I do not know if she was kidding or not. I know her father and, personally, agree with the speculation that he is a hybrid. His behaviors are highly suggestive of a being out of place in human society. Jackie claims to be able to read her children's minds (question thirteen); this may or may not be a completely serious response. Both Mike and Jackie are interested in outer space in general (question sixteen), especially Mike who is a self-proclaimed "sci-fi fanatic" and avid reader of space science news. The rest of the family goes along for the ride, especially the daughter who loves *Star Trek, Star Wars,* and *Space Battleship Yamato* (*Star Blazers* to American audiences). Neither child is interested in UFOs or aliens.

Mike and Jackie both have great personal charisma (question nineteen), acknowledging it in the other while denying it for themselves. Mike suffers from chronic sinusitis (question twenty-one) but gave no explanation why. He also works best at night and with little sleep (question twenty-two), probably as a result of his demanding profession. Jackie had an "unseen" little sister before her younger sibling was born (question twenty-six). Was this precognition or just wish fulfillment of a child's active imagination? Finally, both Mike and Jackie are employed in professions that directly assist other people (question thirty). Altogether, this test as well is negative for the Montgomerys (with the possible exception of Jackie's father).

I must admit, I was a little surprised at the negative results of both questionnaires. I was under the impression that an alien presence was indeed active in the lives of the Montgomerys. The Flat Water witnesses denied any suggestions of abduction as well. So I didn't identify abductees or hybrids among any of these people. Another waste of time following speculations. Not that I wanted any of these people to be an abductee or hybrid. I was just stunned at how the questions so definitively denied abductions and hybridization among these folks.

There may be a new method by which hybridization can occur, a method specifically aimed at twenty-first century technological societies. Those who are not Rh negative or hubrids may very well be in danger of becoming "digitally hybridized." It is a possibility I explored in a short story called "The Screen People," in which iPads and cellular phones mentally altered their users:

> I do not accept—in fact, I cannot believe—that the LCD screens to which the general population are so attached arose, ultimately, from terrestrial technology. Yes, I have bought in to the conspiracy theory that our present-day computers owe their existence to reverse-engineered technology retrieved from crashed UFOs. That's right, I'm talking about Roswell, and any other crashed flying saucer story you can find on that alien invention, the Internet. You can read about this in *The Day After Roswell* by Philip Corso and in books by other ufologists on the same subject; it's not like somebody just confabulated this conspiracy! The screens that people are constantly watching are not the only technology the government and private industry engineered from E.T. tech.
>
> But it is not those other technologies that have me so frightened (dare I say madly terrified) as those portable LCD screens. For I have seen human behavior so altered by these damned invaders that I now fear for the survival of a sizable proportion of what was once the human population. I have no doubt that minds alien and calculating planned this fate for us eons ago.

> The Screen People are not people. There have been those who joke that Screen People are zombies, the shambling undead that are currently so popular in our entertainment culture. But I take that metaphor much more seriously than those who have placed its proclamation as a bumper sticker onto their automobiles. No, I do not believe that the Screen People are literal zombies. I believe they are something far worse. They are the empty husks of what used to be human beings with minds that are now filled with the will of the aliens invading our planet. For when I look into the eyes of the Screen People I find no soul peering back, no personal consciousness, no center of awareness, no singular intelligence—only the blank stare of the biological robot, programmed to behave as mindless servant to the aliens.
>
> The Screen People are the other. I admit my xenophobia freely, for what does that word mean but "fear of the other"? I could no more empathize with a Screen Person than I could with a pocket calculator—probably less, in fact, since the pocket calculator most often provides a useful, helpful service.

Even though "The Screen People" is a science fiction/horror story, much of what I wrote reads like one of the conclusions in this very book! And I am not the only one to have this frightening notion. George Noory included it (in far more detail) in his novel, *Night Talk*:

> The invaders realized that people born during the electronic age are not evolving the same as past generations because their brains are wired differently. And they know how to use it to their advantage . . . These invaders from wherever the hell they flew in from know that people who have been electronically conditioned rather than through intimate contact with family and friends can be left socially isolated without the training that makes them comfortable as co-workers, friends, and lovers . . . The invaders have started making their move now because we have advanced so much electronically that we have made it easy for them to shape our minds. They are doing the shaping by subliminal messages generated through the Internet . . . They know that the addiction to social media gives them the easiest way to shape young brains (Noory 2016: 325–326).

Though Noory is spinning fiction himself, I have to wonder if his idea of social media "brainwashing" the next generation with subliminal messages in digital form on the Internet came from the material on *Coast to Coast AM.* It is a conspiracy theory that might just be right.

I am still flummoxed by the notion that hubrids (human in every way but capable of telepathy) could survive the great environmental changes taking place, which I believe will lead to eventual nuclear annihilation sometime between 2030 and 2050. As I asked before: Why hybridize a population only to inherit a dead planet? To me, it does not make any sense and I doubt if it ever will.

CHAPTER 8

CHAPTER 8
We Are *All* Abductees

(by David)

In 1965, I read Georges Ohsawa's popular macrobiotic diet book, *You Are All Sanpaku*. Although I've never reread it, the book had a lasting impression on me. I found the core premise startling—shocking even—and unbelievable at the same time, which is also how I view the UFO phenomenon. Although it's been over fifty years, I still recall the book's basic message and the effect it had on me. Ohsawa claimed that anyone who had the condition known in Japan as "Sanpaku" (meaning the whites of their eyes are visible below or above the iris) was suffering from physical, psychological, and spiritual imbalance and was doomed to a horrible fate. The good news was that the condition could be corrected by adjusting the person's diet. The shocking part of all this is that the author claimed that most people have this condition, thus the title *You Are All Sanpaku*, which can be interpreted as "You're all doomed." What I found paradigm-shattering about this premise was that it took a fringy conspiracy theory sort of idea (Sanpaku), and said it applies to almost everyone.

The reason I bring up this admittedly wacky book and its hard-to-swallow ideas is that it reminds me very much of my own current view on alien abduction. The common wisdom among ufologists is that a small percentage of the population has been abducted and of that select group, a smaller percentage consciously recalls some portion of the abduction experience. I've seen all sorts of numbers but for the sake of argument, two percent is a good number. That's what a 2002 Roper poll commissioned by the Sci-Fi Channel found: that two percent of the population say they or an acquaintance have had an encounter with an alien life form, according to the findings posted at www.ufoevidence.org/documents/doc989.htm. Let's say that two percent of the population has been abducted by aliens, and maybe half of them remember it without the help of hypnotic regression. That's the consensus view. My personal suspicion of the extent of alien abduction among the population is much more radical than this conservative estimate. I'm like a ufological Georges

Ohsawa. I think it is within the realm of possibility that every human being on Earth is subject to periodic monitoring by and interaction with aliens. That a full one hundred percent of us are abducted at regular intervals throughout our lives. If I wrote a book about this, the title would have to be *We Are All Abductees*. Such an extreme position will no doubt appear ridiculous and unacceptable to many ufologists, let alone the average unconcerned citizen. But that's my current operating theory. Prove me wrong.

So I have this hunch that all humans have alien encounters throughout their lives and regularly interact with aliens and other denizens of alternate dimensions but that most people have no memory of these events. Those who do remember only do so because they have faulty blocking mechanisms that allow fragmentary memories of these uncanny experiences to leak through into their normal consciousness. That's what the two percent really represents: the small minority of abductees who have faulty memory-blocking mechanisms and thus recall some part of their alien encounters. I can't say if the blocking mechanism is something imposed by the aliens as a way of keeping us docile—ignorant and in the dark—or if it's an instinctual protective measure taken by our subconscious minds to shield our conscious minds from having to relive terrifying episodes of psychic abuse and physical assault. My guess is that the blocking mechanism is very effective but not perfect. Were it perfect, none of us would remember anything about our alien encounters, and UFO reports would not exist.

This radical theory becomes more acceptable if you allow yourself to entertain the possibility that not only the UFO phenomenon but the entirety of human existence itself is an unfathomable mystery about which we will never have a full understanding. The appearance of an orderly, rational world around us that is ruled by predictable scientific laws is—possibly—an illusion that our collective minds create out of the infinite seas of chaos that surround us in this unknowable multiverse. This is what is popularly called "The Matrix" view of reality. We live our lives in a false dream, an illusion. Absolute reality is nothing like the average person's view of what is happening in this universe, on this planet, during the course of their days and nights. Perhaps the real message behind alien contact is that we humans, with our puny minds and frail bodies, have no idea of what reality actually is, nor do we understand the terrible fragility of our position in this bizarre, indifferent cosmos.

In this conspiracy theory view of the universe, humans are the slave-like subjects of all powerful alien overlords who rule humanity with an iron fist. They direct our actions, manage our relationships, and breed our hybrid offspring. We sleepwalk through our lives, most of us never suspecting that we are owned; we are—as Charles Fort put it in his classic 1919 work, *The Book of the Damned*—"property." They intrude into the dark corners of our waking lives, invade our dreams, and move around the furniture of our memories, shaping the content of our very existence, while stealing minerals from our Earth, tissues from our bodies, and emotions from our hearts.

I believe that the convenient separation of what is thought of as the "real" physical universe of time, space, and matter from the "unreal" psychic realm of mind, dreams, imagination, memory, and spirit is an artificial construct fostered by our culture and does not adequately represent reality. Aliens and other paranormal entities approach us across a broad band of the Reality-to-Fantasy spectrum and forcefully take command of our bodies and our minds. Not only does ufology not make any sense, there's a very real possibility that reality itself does not make any sense. The so-called physical reality of space, matter, energy, and time may be purely a mental construct, while psychic realms, which are commonly thought to be the product of imagination, may represent the true domain of human existence. And that domain, I suspect, is one where aliens are the apex predators and we are but small, helpless creatures upon whom they prey with impunity.

I confess that's a pretty grim outlook, one I'm sure many ufologists will not warmly embrace. But it very well could be the truth of the matter. Is there any way to prove it to everyone's satisfaction? No, there's not. Is there any way to disprove it to my satisfaction? Again, the answer is no. You can't prove a negative. The most hardened cynic is unable to prove that alien abduction does not exist, nor that it does not affect all humans. No matter what evidence the deniers of Universal Abduction trot out to demonstrate that I am a fool for adopting this theory, I will assure them their hard, scientific "facts" are merely illusion: a holographic projection, a clever screen memory, or the echo of a whisper heard in a dream.

What the data from public polls about UFOs and aliens really tell us is that a small fraction of humans are able to remember portions of their alien abductions, in spite of a mechanism commonly seen in witnesses that works to mask the phenomenon by making them forget the experience. The two percent cited above is actually a measure of the degree to which the blocking mechanism is faulty. The poll data tells us nothing about the larger population of humans that have been abducted but do not recall anything about the experience. Because they do not remember it, they do not report it, and they go uncounted. That larger population of silent abductees could be twenty-five percent of all humans, fifty percent, even one hundred percent.

"How could that be?" you might well ask. How could that make sense? Well, one way it could make sense is if so-called aliens are actually a part of us humans: if they, in a symbiotic relationship with us, form the entire organism. They might be a part of our life cycle, somewhat analogous to the pupa and the butterfly. These seem like two different creatures to the casual observer, but in reality the one springs from the other. Perhaps it's like that with humans and aliens, with one only existing because the other exists in league with it. Or they may be an artificial control system that guides us through the multiverse, engaging in constant course corrections, keeping us headed in a desired direction. I don't know. I have no answers, only questions. That describes the state of ufology. It is myriad questions with very few answers. No scenario involving aliens is too far out to be worth considering. The subject calls for a completely open mind, one which can entertain multiple conflicting viewpoints. Unfortunately, I don't have much faith that humanity is up to the task of understanding the UFO phenomenon or of solving its mysteries, but we have to try. Our very survival may be at stake.

CHAPTER 9

CHAPTER 9
Oregon's Area 51

(by Jordan)

> In the councils of government, we must guard against the acquisition of unwarranted influence, whether sought or unsought, by the military industrial complex. The potential for the disastrous rise of misplaced power exists and will persist.
>
> —President Dwight D. Eisenhower, 1961

I met Frank at the UFO Festival in McMinnville. He overheard me speaking with my friend about Evergreen Aviation and the company's connection to ufology. Now that Evergreen Aviation has filed for bankruptcy and is out of business, except for the museum, Frank felt the time was finally safe to tell his story of working for Evergreen and some of the things he heard and saw while employed for the company. We'd planned to meet a week later at the Hotel Oregon bar.

Frank is a sixty-five-year-old retired USAF who worked closely with the Evergreen management for more than thirty-five years. He was fired at sixty after he became disabled and could not keep up with the workload. Frank received no unemployment insurance and no disability benefits. Evergreen gave him nothing after his long and productive career.

"In the beginning," he began, taking a sip from his micro-brew, "it was just Evergreen Helicopters."

"When was that?" I asked.

"That was back in 1960, when it was founded," he replied. "Then there was Air America and the CIA in secret bombing missions in Laos, back before the Vietnam War was declared. That was in 1964, and 1965. Air America was later bought up by Evergreen Aviation, which was founded in 1975. Hell, Richard Nixon commended Air America employees—how's that for an endorsement?

"You want a timeline on these bastards?" he asked.

"Of course," I replied. "However you want to do this."

"I'll do it any way you want, just keep me a secret."

"No problem," I replied.

"Okay, then. Here it is. In 1980, Evergreen flew the Shah of Iran from Panama to Egypt, just hours before Tehran delivered an extradition request from Panama."

This confused me and all I could ask was, "Why?"

"The Shah was a business partner," he replied. "And the CIA wanted him back in Tehran. The CIA and Evergreen worked together from the beginning and until the company filed Chapter 11." He took another sip of beer before proceeding. "In 1981, Evergreen helicopters were involved in the repair of war-damaged power lines in El Salvador, and the helicopter pilots picked up CIA operatives. Then in 1982, it came out that Evergreen was connected to death squads and other human rights abuses in El Salvador—big surprise, huh? They were also running drugs for the CIA! In 1983, Evergreen delivered twenty-two tons of small arms to a Honduran military base.

"Evergreen's boss was named Delford M. Smith. Have you read *The Evergreen Story*?"

"Only the salient parts," I admitted.

"That should be enough," he replied. "Just go through the book and read what Smith himself said. Really, you should just list a number of his sayings. The Reader will gain a real understanding of that man from his platitudes."

"I'll do that," I promised.

"Good. I remember one time in the boardroom Smith was practically foaming at the mouth, he was so mad. 'Make me more money!' he yelled." Frank shook his head before continuing. "Okay, where was I? Right, 1988. Smith's business companion worked for the CIA to provide jobs and cover to foreign nationals taken out of other countries and brought to the United States.

"Then there was Dean," he said, hanging his head and shaking it. Frank took a huge gulp of his beer. "Dean Clinton Moss was an Evergreen pilot. While flying from Utah to Texas he mysteriously died from internal bleeding in the stomach. And get this—the coroner, Blalack, ruled Dean's death was homicide. I don't know why they killed him."

"They?" I asked.

"Evergreen," he replied with a concealed beer belch.

I was deeply shocked and said so.

"Look it up," he said, continuing. "Then back in the early '90s Evergreen shipped missiles to Israel. In 2002, the company sent flights to Afghanistan. And then in 2004,—get this—Evergreen actually profited from the Iraq War. They sent cargo to Iraq and received forty percent of the $570 million operating revenue.

"Smith was obsessed with money," he continued. "Yeah, the last year I worked for Evergreen, 2005, $600 thousand from the Aviation and Space Museum was funneled to Evergreen and to Smith personally. Can you f---ing believe that?" Frank nodded knowingly. "I'm telling you, man. It's all true. My back and knees went out at pretty much the same time and I was left disabled. Hence this damned contraption." He shook his walker angrily. "I was fired, like I said, and I got no unemployment insurance and no disability. I am now living on a meager inheritance from my mother. So 2005, is the last bit I got on my own. But I still had a friend working for Evergreen who kept me up to date."

I nodded as I jotted down what Frank was disclosing to me.

"Evergreen flew Bill O'Reilly to Kuwait. I never figured that one out. Also in 2006, Amnesty International pronounced allegations that Evergreen was flying planes for extraordinary rendition."

I looked up, surprised. "You mean the extraordinary renditions that—"

"That brought Arabs to other countries where the CIA tortured them beyond the laws of this nation!" Frank's beer arrived and he finished a quarter of it in a couple large drafts. "Then in 2008, Evergreen president Tom Wiggins offered to provide mercenaries to detain troublemakers at Oregon voting sites."

This truly baffled me. "Why?"

Frank shrugged. "Racism. The man couldn't stand the fact that our country was electing a black president."

I stammered a bit, confused. "But Oregon voting is by mail!"

Frank exploded into sardonic laughter. "Exactly! It was a bizarre offer that was completely irrational.

"In 2009," he continued, "Evergreen received a $158 million contract to supply the Air Force with helicopters, which probably ended up in the Middle East."

"Bad year," I commented. "That's when I was let go from my job at university."

"Bad year for me, too," he said, drinking. "I was still learning how to be poor and survive. But karma got that Smith SOB. In 2011, Evergreen's huge debts—half a billion dollars!—caught up with them and the company started to tank. Soon after they filed for bankruptcy."

As I finished jotting down my notes I realized that I had not asked him one question referring to secret weapons tests, chemtrails, and UFOs.

"Secret weapons?" he asked, rubbing his beard. "I don't know about that. The researchers did work on drones. You can find that in *The Evergreen Story*. It's reported in there with a sickening pride."

I found the section on UAVs (Unmanned Aerial Vehicles) on pages 249–251 in the book. Evergreen planned to use A-20 Insight UAVs for "ocean fishing surveillance." However, "following the attack of September 11, 2001, it was converted into the Scan Eagle UAV system, which is flown in military operations by Boeing." The use of drones was indeed promoted with pride.

"Dr. Coldwell," Frank murmured.

I looked up from my notes. "Coldwell?"

"DrLeonardColdwell.com. Check it. You want secret shit? This is it. Chemtrails."

I was a little shocked, having written a short story about Evergreen using the name "Conifer" in which the company prepares a jet for a chemtrail mission. "Really?"

"If you believe Coldwell and a lot of other folks," he replied.

"What's in the chemtrails?" I asked.

Frank drank his pint of beer and looked off to some unseen sky. "Aluminum and barium," he said, "but I'm not sure about this. Coldwell got the story from a drunk pilot. Supposedly the aluminum and barium have caused respiratory illnesses in populations that have had chemtrails dumped on them. Also, it acidifies the soil. And supposedly this is all for weather control. I don't know. But a lot of folks say they do know, so don't take my skepticism to heart."

I literally scratched my head. "And UFOs?"

Frank looked at me and smiled. "Oh, yeah. We had a downed craft."

I was astonished. "You gotta be kidding."

Frank laughed. "Of course I am. I just had to mess with you!"

I had my computer with me so I was already searching the Internet. "Woah!" I exclaimed. "Listen to this, Frank. In 2013, a huge long metallic UFO was sighted over the Evergreen Aviation and Space Museum and reported to MUFON. I know those guys, Tom and Keith. They're excellent investigators. Here, check out the photo."

Frank shrugged. "Yeah, it looks like a UFO, meaning I have no idea what the hell it is."

"It's intriguing," I said. I read the witness's statement to MUFON:

> Hello, I was visiting the Evergreen Aviation and Space Museum in McMinnville, Oregon, and I have a couple of pictures I would like you to take a look at. Look at the pickup in the background in picture one, and then where it is in picture two, the pictures were taken about two seconds apart and I did not see any aircraft flying in the area the entire time I was there.
>
> But picture two clearly has an object in the upper middle. I heard nothing but highway traffic no airplanes or helicopters and did not hear anything from the object. I noticed the object later looking at the photo and thought that is a UFO.

"Well, that's the only UFO I ever heard of," he said. "I never saw one and I never heard any of the pilots talking about them. Of course, they wouldn't have been able to. Smith would have fired them." He finished his beer. "And then that greedy old bastard died in 2014. I think inside I cheered . . ."

"So," I said, "I can't really call Evergreen 'Oregon's Area 51.'"

Frank shook his head. "Oh, no. You sure as hell can. There were several instances in which I realized just how much security Evergreen had working for them, maybe even Blackwater. There were areas that were definitely off limits. No one but the 'spooks,' the high-security engineers, etcetera, were permitted in those areas. I heard about the boss's collection of weapons, but I never got to see it. At least some parts of Evergreen Aviation were similar to Area 51. When they were working on the militarized UAVs that was a big secret. I only found out about that stuff later. Still, if the chemtrail conspiracy is at all true and if your UFO really did fly over the museum, then it starts to sound an awful lot like the American conspiracy theorists' version of Area 51, but I'm not going to call it that. You can, of course. It's your book."

I laughed. Frank was exhausted. I thanked him for the interview and all the amazing information he had rattled off to me. As he was leaving he reminded me, "Print Smith's quotes from that book, man. His own words are as distasteful as his actions."

I again promised to include Smith's platitudes, shook Frank's hand and helped him to his walker. I never saw or spoke with Frank again. He changed his email address, Facebook page, and phone number. But I had his advice and, apparently, a book that held condemnation of Delford M. Smith and his company, written in Smith's own words. Later, I began a list from pages eighteen and nineteen in *The Evergreen Story* and compiled it for his self-conviction below:

- Don't come home without a deal.
- To err is human, but forgiveness is not our company policy.
- Options are to get—not to give.
- We are in business for two reasons—fun and profit.

If there's no profit, it ain't no fun.

- We must continue to have a healthy discontent for the present.
- Performance is the only thing that counts.
- God gave us life; we owe him our best performance.
- Commit to profit in operations. Sales is the engine that runs the company.

Everything is about money and making more and more. That is what lay squirming in the heart of Delford M. Smith. "I was raised with Benjamin Franklin's Virtues for Living, the Ten Commandments, and the Napoleon Hill Philosophy," he proclaimed.

While visiting the Evergreen Aviation and Space Museum's bizarre rooftop 747 waterslides, I noticed the Ten Commandments written in huge letters on the wall. Interestingly, Commandment 6, "Thou Shalt Not Kill" was changed to "Thou Shalt Not Murder." I had to wonder about this. Clearly, Smith knew damn well that his company had killed in the past and was doing so in the present Mideast War. The reworded Commandment seems to be a personal absolution: that murder is wrong but killing is business.

The last of Franklin's Virtues for Living reads:

13. HUMILITY
IMITATE JESUS AND SOCRATES.

Everything that Delford M. Smith stood for is in direct contradiction to Franklin's Thirteenth Virtue. Jesus never would have approved of all the life lost due to Evergreen's clandestine activities. And Socrates would rather take hemlock than a gun's cock. But this chapter is not meant as a condemnation of Delford M. Smith, as much as Frank would like it to be. *The Evergreen Story,* written by Bill Yenne, tells a largely positive tale of a humanitarian company run by enduring virtues. Still, the endorsements that appear several times on and inside the book are a reminder of the kind of people with whom Smith was working and his political ties to the far-right:

> I want you to know how truly impressed I am by what you have done with your life. The business success properly speaks for itself. You are universally admired for that. But your being one of a "thousand points of light" says even more.
>
> —George Herbert Walker Bush
> 41st President of the United States

A "thousand points of light"? Bush forty-one might just as well have been speaking of UFOs! And if Delford M. Smith was a "point of light," then we live in a very dark universe indeed!

Smith was also praised by Senator John McCain on becoming a self-made man.

Of course George Bush, Sr. was once head of the CIA. Smith was keen on nabbing those contracts. Through most of its history, Evergreen worked very closely with and for the CIA. My guess is that there was a lot more UFO activity around the Evergreen complex for all the decades it operated.

A grumpy Jordy stands in front of Evergreen's vineyard and the museum with a 747 on the roof, featuring thrilling water slides. *Photograph by Mark Madland, 2015.*

As a UFO researcher I have to consider the possibility that there is a direct connection between the Trent sighting on May 11, 1950, and the presence of Evergreen in the same small city in Oregon's Willamette Valley. Was this the reason that Evergreen Aviation made its HQ in McMinnville precisely because of the presence of UFOs? The installation itself is in the wide open, apparently totally exposed to any prying eyes. Maybe not the best place for such high-level secrets?

I have reviewed the photograph of a UFO above Evergreen that was submitted to MUFON and I can only say it is an unknown. It does have what appears to be a metallic gleam to it and seems like the object, with a jet in the foreground, was some distance away from the museum when the photo was shot. If this analysis is correct then the UFO was pretty big, at least as large as a 747. UFOs are often seen over military installations. Was Evergreen attracting UFOs? Are they still present in McMinnville?

As I was arranging our private club's (Salem Low-Flying Triangle) ufology library I found, to my astonishment, a book that connected Evergreen with UFOs. The same author who had written *The Evergreen Story*, Bill Yenne, had also written a large coffee table-sized book entitled *U.F.O. Evaluating the Evidence.* I couldn't believe it. The missing link from Evergreen to UFOs had been sitting on our bookshelf! A quick check for the works of Bill Yenne on Amazon revealed a plethora of books, including novels and non-fiction, ranging from aeronautics to World War II history to beer. His only published book on UFOs is the one I already own. Still, the UFO connection to Evergreen seems almost a conspicuous synchronicity.

But we may never know. Smith is dead. Evergreen is bankrupt. All that remains are the giant's toys that Smith left in his museum and on the museum's lawns, as well as a vineyard in front, dutifully tended to by migrant workers. Was Evergreen Oregon's Area 51? If so then it was a very lame Area 51.

Conclusion
In Dubio Verum Est

(by Jordan)

> Something happened yesterday [July 22, 2016]—I think that it was 'THEM' again! It actually happened the night before, but have felt weird/sick ever since! I decided to lie on the couch for a while around 10:00 p.m. to watch a DVD, but the next thing that I remember is waking up . . . looked up and around the living room, but did not know where I was. It was as if I had never seen this place before. I felt terrified and sick to my stomach, also felt dehydrated for some reason!! I got up and went to lie down on my bed, looked at the clock . . . it said 12:45 a.m., and then???? I don't even recall laying my head on the pillow. Next thing I know it was morning, around 5:30 a.m. Probably nothing, maybe not them? I don't know really!!? Just a strange couple of days.
>
> —Corina Saebels
> Author of *The Collectors*

Ufology should proceed with doubt if it is to survive the millions of drones in our skies and the masterful computer graphics on our screens. We should expect to see an increase in not just "unidentified" but truly "unidentifiable" flying objects, as well as a concomitant rise in IFOs (Identified Flying Objects) when research discovers mundane explanations for seemingly strange phenomena. We must not believe but accept or deny evidence for the existence of UFOs. Belief dispels doubt and without doubt ufology becomes a useless enterprise, especially now in the twenty-first century.

A modest and doubtful proposal: Hydrogen atoms, noted Carl Sagan, evolved over billions of years into a self-aware Universe. If we and other species are the consciousness of the Universe then what of the unconscious? We must also be the living unconsciousness of the Universe. We dream, and through us the Universe dreams. Maybe a dreaming Universe produces the paranormal activity our species experiences from UFOs and aliens to ghosts and bizarre creatures—they all share a common origin in dreams. Should the self-aware Universe stop dreaming, these strange phenomena would possibly disappear because consciousness needs the unconscious every time it sleeps. We are locked together, the conscious and the unconscious Universe, and the paranormal phenomena continue unsolvable.

So doubt our eyes. Doubt our memories. Doubt our dreams. Doubt our perceptions. Doubt everything we have read in any book and seen on any screen. Doubt the experts. Doubt this book. Do not be afraid to say, "I don't know." Unless we solve the UFO enigma very soon, uncertainty will forever remain the alpha and omega of ufology—I think.

Truth lies in doubt.

David's Doubts

Belief is indeed the enemy. For belief implies certainty, and there can be no certainty when you're dealing with true UFOs—the unidentified, and unidentifiable. If the evidence in a case convinces you that a reported aerial object is an aircraft or a drone or a star or a bird, accept that with certainty. But if an object cannot be identified as some mundane thing, then refrain from believing anything about it. Accept it as an unsolved mystery, gather what information you can about it, and move on to the next report.

I'm not expecting the UFO mystery to be solved in my lifetime, if ever. Science as presently practiced only explains physical phenomena—that which can be observed and measured in the light of day. But UFOs, aliens, and other specters dwell in the darkness. Not physical darkness, but spiritual darkness. Science can't shine a light on them, and cannot take their measure. They exist—and likely will remain—just beyond our grasp.

> We must not look at goblin men,
> We must not buy their fruits:
> Who knows upon what soil they fed
> Their hungry thirsty roots?
>
> —Excerpt from Christina Rossetti's 1859 poem "Goblin Market"

Glossary

(by Jordan)

Amino acid: The "building block" of proteins; a protein is a string of amino acids that have contorted into their lowest energy state conformation.

Codon: A three-nucleotide sequence that codes for specific amino acids during translation.

DNA: Deoxyribonucleic acid, the double helix that codes for every protein in an organism. Most of the DNA structure is composed of introns, regions that appear to assist in the action of exons (the nucleic acids that code for amino acids during translation).

Genetic Drift: One of the four forces of evolution, genetic drift is a random force that separates potential breeding populations, resulting in the decrease of genetic variation within a breeding population and the increase of genetic variation between breeding populations.

Mutation: Any change in the genetic code resulting in the translation of altered proteins. A "frameshift mutation" occurs when DNA or RNA loses or gains one or more nucleic acids, resulting in an altered code.

Nucleic acid: Coding molecule in the cell nucleus (i.e., DNA and RNA) as opposed to amino acids, which comprise proteins. A nucleotide is any one of the four coding bases in DNA: adenine (A), thymine (T), cytosine (C), and guanine (G); A always bonds with T and C with G. In RNA, uracil (U) binds with A instead of T with A.

Plasma: A high-energy electromagnetic field that strips the electrons from atoms and radiates intense heat and light. Possible propulsion system for at least some UFOs and orbs.

Ribosome: A large protein complex in the cytoplasm that translates nucleic acids into amino acids and, thus, proteins.

RNA: Ribonucleic acid comprised of a single strand of nucleotides including uracil (U), adenine, guanine, and cytosine. Messenger RNA (mRNA) leaves the nucleus after transcription and is translated by a ribosome into amino acids. Some form of self-replicating RNA was the ancestor of DNA.

Transcription: The coding from double-stranded DNA to single-stranded RNA, after which the Messenger RNA (mRNA) leaves the cell nucleus and is translated by a ribosome in the cytoplasm into amino acids and proteins.

Translation: The process by which a ribosome uses RNA to build strings of amino acids and proteins.

Bibliography

Adamski, George. *Flying Saucers Farewell.* New York, NY: Abelard-Schuman, Inc., 1961.

Adamski, George. *Inside the Space Ships.* New York, NY: Abelard-Schuman, Inc., 1955.

Alexander, John B. *UFOs: Myths, Conspiracies, and Realities*. New York, NY: Thomas Dunne Books, 2011.

Allen, W. Gordon. *Space-Craft from Beyond Three Dimensions: A New Vista of the Entirety from Which Emerges the UFO.* New York, NY: Exposition Press, 1959.

Allingham, Cedric. *Flying Saucer from Mars.* New York, NY: British Book Centre, 1955.

Angelucci, Orfeo. *Concrete Evidence.* Scotia, NY: Arcturus Book Service, 1983.

Angelucci, Orfeo. *Million Year Prophecy.* Scotia, NY: Arcturus Book Service, 1983.

Angelucci, Orfeo. *The Secret of the Saucers*. Amherst, WI: Amherst Press, 1955.

Arnold, Kenneth and Ray Palmer. *The Coming of the Saucers: A Documentary Report on Sky Objects that Have Mystified the World.* Amherst, WI: Privately published by the authors, 1952.

Barker, David. *Alien Autopsy Barbecue*. Salem, OR: Golden Posterity Press, 2013.

Barker, David. *Cigar Shaped Craft*. Salem, OR: End of Time Productions, 1985.

Barker, David. *Frank Scully and the Legend of the Crashed Saucers*. Salem, OR: New Etherian Press, 1985.

Barker, David. *The Reality Hoax—UFOs, Alien Beings, and the Conspiracy to Deceive*. Salem, OR: New Etherian Press, 1985.

Barker, David. *Scenarios of Alien Visitation*. Salem, OR: Saucers Unlimited, 1985.

Barker, David and Jordan Hofer. *Chupacabra Chalupa—Bizarro Science Fiction Stories*. Salem, OR: Golden Posterity Press, 2013.

Barker, Gray. *Gray Barker's Book of Adamski*. Pt. Pleasant, WV: New Saucerian Books, 2014.

Barker, Gray. *They Knew Too Much about Flying Saucers*. New York, NY: Tower, 1967.

Barry, Bill. *Ultimate Encounter*. New York, NY: Pocket Books, 1978.

Beckley, Timothy Green. *UFOs Among the Stars*. New Brunswick, NJ: Global Communications, 1992.

Bender, Albert K. and Gray Barker. *Flying Saucers and the Three Men*. London: Neville Spearman, 1963.

Bennett, Colin. *Looking for Orthon; The Story of George Adamski, the First Flying Saucer Contactee, and How He Changed the World*. New York, NY: Paraview Press, 2001.

Bergier, Jacque and the Editors of INFO. *Extraterrestrial Intervention: The Evidence*. Chicago, IL: Henry Regnery Company, 1974.

Berlitz, Charles and William L. Moore. *The Roswell Incident*. New York, NY: Grosset & Dunlap, 1980.

Bethurum, Truman. *Aboard a Flying Saucer*. Los Angeles, CA: DeVorss & Co., 1954.

Bethurum, Truman. *Truman Bethurum's Personal Scrapbook*. Scotia, NY: Robert C. Girard, 1982.

Bethurum, Truman and Timothy Green Beckley. *Messages from the People of the Planet Clarion: The True Experiences of Truman Bethurum*. New Brunswick, NJ: 1995.

Binder, Otto O. *Flying Saucers Are Watching Us.* New York, NY: Belmont Books, 1968.

Birnes, William J. *Aliens in America: A UFO Hunter's Guide to Extraterrestrial Hotspots Across the U.S.* Avon, MA: Adams Media, 2010.

Blum, Ralph and Judy Blum. *Beyond Earth: Man's Contact with UFOs.* New York, NY: Bantam Books, 1974.

Blumrich, Josef F. *The Spaceships of Ezekiel.* New York, NY: Bantam Books, 1974.

The Book of Space Ships and Their Relationship with Earth, by the God of a Planet Near Earth and Others. Clarkesburg, WV: Saucerian Publications, n.d.

Brown, Courtney. *Cosmic Explorers: Scientific Remote Viewing, Extraterrestrials, and a Message for Mankind.* New York, NY: Signet, 2000.

Brown, Courtney. *Cosmic Voyage: A Scientific Discovery of Extraterrestrials Visiting Earth.* New York, NY: Penguin Books USA Inc., 1996.

Bryan, C. D. B. *Close Encounters of the Fourth Kind.* New York, NY: Penguin Books USA Inc., 1995.

Carlton, Jeff. "CIA Documents Reveal Details About Secretive Air America Airline." *Huffington Post* (2011): www.huffingtonpost.com.

Clark, Jerome and Loren Coleman. *The Unidentified: Notes Towards Solving the UFO Mystery.* New York, NY: Warner Paperback Library, 1975.

Conroy, Ed. *Report on Communion.* New York, NY: Avon Books, 1989.

Contreras, Jessie A. *The Short and Simple Practical Guide on How to Summon UFO's* [sic]. Los Angeles, CA: Jessie A. Contreras, 2013.

Cooper, Milton William. *Behold a Pale Horse.* Flagstaff, AZ: Light Technology Publishing, 1991.

Corso, Col. Philip J. (Ret.) *The Day after Roswell.* New York, NY: Pocket Books, 1997.

Darwin, Charles. *On the Origin of Species*. Cambridge, MA: Harvard University Press, 2003.

David, Jay. *The Flying Saucer Reader*. New York, NY: The New American Library, Inc., 1967.

Dawkins, Richard. *The Magic of Reality*. New York, NY: Free Press, 2011.

Dembeck, Chet. *We Are Not Alone and They Are Not Our Friends*. Baltimore, MD: Chet Dembeck and Publisher of One, 2012.

Dimond, Brother Michael. *UFOs: Demonic Activity & Elaborate Hoaxes Meant to Deceive Mankind*. Fillmore, NY: Most Holy Family Monastery, 2009.

Dolan, Richard M. and Bryce Zabel. *A.D. After Disclosure*. Rochester, NY: Keyhole Publishing Company, 2010.

Downing, Barry. *The Bible and Flying Saucers*. New York, NY: Marlowe & Company, 1997.

Druffel, Ann and D. Scott Rogo. *The Tujunga Canyon Contacts*. Englewood Cliffs, NJ: Prentice-Hall, Inc., 1980.

Edwards, Frank. *Flying Saucers—Here and Now!* New York, NY: Lyle Stuart, 1967.

Edwards, Frank. *Flying Saucers—Serious Business*. New York, NY: Bantam Books, 1966.

Eichar, Donnie. *Dead Mountain: The Untold True Story of the Dyatlov Pass Incident*. San Francisco, CA: Chronicle Books LLC, 2013.

Elders, Lee and Brit Nilsson-Elders. *UFO . . . Contact from the Pleiades, Volume II*. Phoenix, AZ: Genesis III Productions, Inc., 1983.

Elders, Lee J., Brit Nilsson-Elders, and Thomas K. Welch. *UFO: Contact from the Pleiades, Volume I*. Phoenix, AZ: Genesis III Productions, Ltd., 1979.

"Evergreen International Aviation, Inc." www.sourcewatch.org.

Fawcett, Lawrence and Barry J. Greenwood. *Clear Intent: The Government Coverup of the UFO Experience*. Englewood Cliffs, NJ: Prentice-Hall, Inc., 1984.

FBI. "George Adamski File". BUFILE No. 100-395273.

Felber, Ron. *Searchers: A True Story*. New York, NY: St. Martin's Paperbacks, 1995.

Ferguson, William. *My Trip to Mars*. Potomac, MD: Cosmic Study Center, n.d.

Fort, Charles. *The Book of the Damned*. New York, NY: Ace Books,. First published 1919.

Fowler, Raymond. *The Andreasson Affair*. New York, NY: Bantam Books, 1980.

Fowler, Raymond. *The Andreasson Affair, Phase Two*. Englewood Cliffs, NJ: Prentice-Hall, Inc., 1982.

Fowler, Raymond. *The Andreasson Legacy*. New York, NY: Marlowe & Company, 1997.

Fowler, Raymond. *The Watchers: The Secret Design Behind UFO Abduction*. New York, NY: Bantam Books, 1990.

Fowler, Raymond. *The Watchers II*. Newberg, OR: Wild Flower Press, 1995.

Friedman, Stanton T. and Don Berliner. *Crash at Corona: The U.S. Military Retrieval and Cover-Up of a UFO*. New York, NY: Marlowe Company, 1994.

Friedman, Stanton T. and Kathleen Marden. *Captured! The Betty and Barney Hill UFO Experience*. Franklin Lakes, NJ: The Career Press, Inc., 2007.

Fry, Daniel W. *"The White Sands Incident" and "To Men of Earth"* New Combined Edition, n.d.

Fuller, John G. *Aliens in the Skies: The Scientific Rebuttal to the Condon Committee Report*. New York, NY: G.P. Putnam's Sons, 1969.

Fuller, John G. *Incident at Exeter: The Story of Unidentified Flying Objects over America Today*. New York, NY: G.P. Putnam's Sons, 1966.

Fuller, John G. *The Interrupted Journey: Two Lost Hours "Aboard a Flying Saucer."* New York, NY: The Dial Press, 1966.

Gaddis, Vincent H. *Mysterious Fires and Lights*. New York, NY: David McKay Company, Inc., 1967.

Gibbons, Gavin. *On Board the Flying Saucers*. New York, NY: Paperback Library, Inc., 1957.

Good, Timothy. *Alien Update*. New York, NY: Avon Books, 1993.

Green, Gabriel and Warren Smith. *Let's Face the Facts about Flying Saucers*. New York, NY: Popular Library, 1967.

Hampsch, Reverend John H. *Devils and Demons: Fact or Fiction?* Goleta, CA: Queenship Publishing Company, 2002.

Hampsch, Reverend John H. *Poltergeists and Seven Types of Ghosts*. Goleta, CA: Queenship Publishing Company, 2008.

Heard, Gerald. *Is Another World Watching? The Riddle of the Flying Saucers*. New York, NY: Harper & Brothers Publishers, 1951.

Hesemann, Michael and Philip Mantle. *Beyond Roswell: The Alien Autopsy Film, Area 51, & the U.S. Government Coverup of UFOs*. New York, NY: Marlowe & Company, 1997.

Hewes, Hayden and Brad Steiger. *UFO Missionaries Extraordinary*. New York, NY: Pocket Books, 1976.

Hill, Paul R. *Unconventional Flying Objects: A Scientific Analysis*. Charlottesville, VA: Hampton Roads Publishing Company, Inc., 1995.

Hobana, Ion and Julien Weverbergh. *UFO's from Behind the Iron Curtain*. New York, NY: Bantam Books, 1974.

Hodge, Nathan. "Mercenary Firm Offers to 'Detain Troublemakers' on Election Day (Updated)." *Wired*. www.wired.com/2008/11/spooky-defense, 2008.

Hofer, Jordan. *Conifer: Book Two of the Saucerville Trilogy*. Amazon CreateSpace, 2015.

Hofer, Jordan. "An Evolutionary Ufology Hypothesis." *MUFON UFO Journal*, no. 507 (2010): 12.

Hofer, Jordan. *Evolutionary Ufology: A New Synthesis*. Atglen, PA: Schiffer Publishing, Ltd., 2013.

Hofer, Jordan. "From UFO Disbeliever to Believer." *Statesman Journal* (June 23, 2012): Section C, Final Edition.

Hofer, Jordan. *Saucerville*. Portland, OR: Inkwater Press, 2013.

Hofer, Jordan and David Barker. *Little Gray Bastards: The Incessant Alien Presence*. Atglen, PA: Schiffer Publishing, Ltd., 2016.

Hopkins, Budd. *Art, Life and UFOs*. San Antonio, TX: Anomalist Books, 2009.

Hopkins, Budd. *Intruders: The Incredible Visitations at Copley Woods*. New York, NY: Ballantine Books, 1987.

Hopkins, Budd. *Missing Time: A Documented Study of UFO Abductions*. New York, NY: Berkley Books, 1981.

Hopkins, Budd. *Witnessed: The True Story of the Brooklyn Bridge UFO Abductions*. New York, NY: Pocket Books, 1996.

Howe, Linda Moulton. *An Alien Harvest: Further Evidence Linking Animal Mutilations and Human Abductions to Alien Life Forms.* Huntingdon Valley, PA: Linda Moulton Howe Productions, 1989.

Huyghe, Patrick. *The Field Guide to Extraterrestrials.* New York, NY: Avon Books, 1996.

Hymers, Dr. R. L., Jr. and David Shigekawa. *UFO's and Bible Prophecy.* Van Nuys, CA: Bible Voice, Inc., 1976.

Hynek, J. Allen. *The Hynek UFO Report.* New York, NY: Dell, 1977.

Hynek, J. Allen. *The UFO Experience: A Scientific Inquiry*. Chicago, IL: Henry Regnery Company, 1972.

Hynek, J. Allen, Philip J. Imbrogno, and Bob Pratt. *Night Siege: The Hudson Valley UFO Sightings*. St. Paul, MN: Llewellyn Publications, 1998.

Hynek, J. Allen and Jacques Vallee. *The Edge of Reality: A Progress Report on Unidentified Flying Objects.* Chicago, IL: Henry Regnery Company, 1975.

Jacobs, David M. *Secret Life: Firsthand Accounts of UFO Abductions.* New York, NY: Simon & Schuster, 1992.

Jacobs, David M. *The Threat: The Secret Agenda: What the Aliens Really Want and How They Plan to Get It.* New York, NY: Simon & Schuster, 1998.

Jacobs, David Michael. *The UFO Controversy in America.* New York, NY: Signet, 1975.

Jacobs, David M. *UFOs and Abductions: Challenging the Borders of Knowledge.* Lawrence, Kansas: University Press of Kansas, 2000.

Jacobs, David M. *Walking Among Us: The Alien Plan to Control Humanity.* San Francisco, CA: Disinformation Books, 2015.

Jeffries, Benjamin. *Lost in the Darkness: Life Inside the World's Most Haunted Prisons, Hospitals, and Asylums.* Atglen, PA: Schiffer Publishing, Ltd., 2013.

Jessup, M. K. *The Case for the UFO.* New York, NY: The Citadel Press, 1955.

Jessup, M. K. *The Expanding Case for the UFO.* New York, NY: The Citadel Press, 1957.

Jordan, Debbie and Kathy Mitchell. *Abducted!* New York, NY: Dell Publishing, 1994.

Jung, C. G. *Flying Saucers.* New York, NY: MJF Books, 1978.

Kean, Leslie. *UFOs: Generals, Pilots, and Government Officials Go on the Record.* New York, NY: Harmony Books, 2010.

Keel, John A. *The Eighth Tower.* New York, NY: Signet, 1975.

Keel, John A. *The Mothman Prophecies.* New York, NY: Tor, 1991.

Keel, John A. *Our Haunted Planet.* Greenwich, CT: Fawcett Gold Medal, 1971.

Keyhoe, Donald E. *Aliens from Space: The Real Story of Unidentified Flying Objects.* Garden City, NY: Doubleday & Company, Inc., 1973.

Keyhoe, Major Donald. *The Flying Saucers Are Real.* Lexington, KY: CreateSpace, 2012.

Keyhoe, Major Donald E. *Flying Saucers from Outer Space.* New York, NY: Henry Holt and Company, 1953.

Keyhoe, Major Donald E. *The Flying Saucer Conspiracy.* New York, NY: Henry Holt and Company, 1955.

Kinchen, David M. "$50-Million Business Center Set: County to Gain from Lease of Former Long Beach Hospital Site." *Los Angeles Times* (March 2, 1986). Electronic version at http://articles.latimes.com/1986-03-02/realestate/re-1138_1_ground-lease.

Kinder, Gary. *Light Years: An Investigation into the Extraterrestrial Experiences of Eduard Meier.* New York, NY: The Atlantic Monthly Press, 1987.

King, George D.D. *The Flying Saucers: A Report on Flying Saucers, Their Crews and Their Mission to Earth.* Los Angeles, CA: The Aetherius Society, 1964.

Landsburg, Alan and Leonard Nimoy. *In Search of Extraterrestrials.* New York, NY: Bantam Books, 1976.

Larkins, Lisette. *Talking to Extraterrestrials: Communicating with Enlightened Beings.* Charlottesville, VA: Hampton Roads, 2002.

Leir, Roger K. *Alien Implants.* New York, NY: Dell Publishing, 2000.

Leonard, George H. *Somebody Else Is on the Moon.* New York, NY: Pocket Books, 1976.

Lepselter, Susan. *The Resonance of Unseen Things: Poetics, Power, Captivity, and UFOs in the American Uncanny*. Ann Arbor, MI: University of Michigan Press, 2016.

Leslie, Desmond and George Adamski. *Flying Saucers Have Landed.* New York, NY: The British Book Centre, 1953.

Lorenzen, Coral E. *Flying Saucers: The Startling Evidence of the Invasion from Outer Space*. New York, NY: Signet, 1966.

Lorenzen, Coral and Jim Lorenzen. *Encounters with UFO Occupants.* New York, NY: Berkley Medallion, 1976.

Lorenzen, Coral and Jim Lorenzen. *Flying Saucer Occupants.* New York, NY: Signet, 1967.

Lorenzen, Jim and Coral Lorenzen. *UFOs Over the Americas.* New York, NY: Signet, 1968.

Lorenzen, Jim and Coral Lorenzen. *UFOs: The Whole Story.* New York, NY: Signet, 1969.

Mack, John E. *Abduction: Human Encounters with Aliens*. New York, NY: Ballantine Books, 1994.

Mack, John E. *Passport to the Cosmos*. New York, NY: Crown Publishers, 1999.

Maloney, Mack. *UFOs in Wartime*. New York, NY: The Berkeley Publishing Group, 2011.

Mannion, Michael. *Project Mindshift: The Re-education of the American Public Concerning Extraterrestrial Life, 1947–Present.* New York, NY: M. Evans and Company, Inc., 1998.

Marden, Kathleen and Denise Stoner. *The Alien Abduction Files: The Most Startling Cases of Human Alien Contact Ever Reported.* Pompton Plains, NJ: New Page Books, 2013.

Marrs, Jim. *Alien Agenda: Investigating the Extraterrestrial Presence Among Us.* New York, NY: HarperCollinsPublishers, 1997.

McCampbell, James M. *Ufology.* Millbrae, CA: Celestial Arts, 1976.

Menger, Howard. *From Outer Space*. New York, NY: Pyramid Books, 1959.

Menzel, Donald H. and Lyle G. Boyd. *The World of Flying Saucers: A Scientific Examination of a Major Myth of the Space Age.* Garden City, NY: Doubleday & Company, Inc., 1963.

Michel, Aimé. *The Truth about Flying Saucers.* New York, NY: Pyramid Books, 1956.

Mitchell, John. *The Flying Saucer Vision.* New York, NY: Ace, 1967.

Moore, Patrick. *Can You Speak Venusian? A Guide to the Independent Thinkers.* London: Star, 1972.

Moore, William L. *Crashed Saucers: Evidence in Search of Proof.* MUFON Symposium Proceedings, 1985.

Moore, William L. and Stanton T. Friedman. *The Roswell Investigation: New Evidence, New Conclusions & The Roswell Incident: Beginnings of the Cosmic Watergate.* Prescott, AZ: William L. Moore Publications, 1982.

Moore, William L. and Charles Berlitz. *The Philadelphia Experiment: Project Invisibility.* New York, NY: Grosset & Dunlap, 1979.

Moore, William L. *The Roswell Investigation: New Evidence in the Search for a Crashed UFO.* Prescott, AZ: William L. Moore Publications, 1982.

Ohsawa, Georges. *You Are All Sanpaku.* New Hyde Park, NY: University Books. 1965.

Perry, George H., et. al. "Evolutionary genetics of the human Rh blood group system." *Human Genetics* 131 (7) (July 2012): 1205–1216.

Pope, Nick. *Operation Lightning Strike.* London, UK: Simon & Schuster UK Ltd, 2000.

Pope, Nick. *The Uninvited: An Exposé of the Alien Abduction Phenomenon.* New York, NY: Dell Publishing, 1997.

Pope, Nick, John Burroughs, and Jim Penniston. *Encounter in Rendlesham Forest.* New York, NY: St. Martin's Press, 2014.

Psychospy [pseud.]. "All About Boron." *The Groom Lake Desert Rat* (1995). Electronic version at www.ufomind.com/area51/desertrat/1995/dr24/#boron.

Randle, Kevin D. *Case MJ-12: The True Story Behind the Government's UFO Conspiracies.* New York, NY: HarperTorch, 2002.

Randle, Kevin D. *A History of UFO Crashes*. New York, NY: Avon, 1995.

Randle, Kevin D. *Invasion Washington: UFOs Over the Capitol*. New York, NY: HarperCollinsPublishers, 2001.

Randle, Kevin D. *Scientific Ufology*. New York, NY: Avon Books, Inc., 1999.

Randle, Kevin D. *The UFO Casebook*. New York, NY: Warner Books, Inc., 1989.

Randle, Kevin D., Russ Estes, and William P. Cone. *The Abduction Enigma*. New York, NY: Tom Doherty Associates, Inc., 1999.

Randle, Kevin D. and Donald R. Schmitt. *The Truth about the UFO Crash at Roswell*. New York, NY: Avon, 1994.

Randle, Kevin D., Capt., U.S.A.F.R., and Donald R. Schmitt. *UFO Crash at Roswell*. New York, NY: Avon, 1991.

Randles, Jenny. *UFO Retrievals: The Recovery of Alien Spacecraft*. London, UK: Blandford, 1995.

Redfern, Nick. *Bloodline of the Gods*. Wayne, NJ: New Page Books, 2015.

Redfern, Nick. *Close Encounters of the Fatal Kind*. Pompton Plains, NJ: New Page Books, 2014.

Redfern, Nick. *Women In Black*. Lisa Hagan Books, 2016.

Reeve, Bryant and Helen Reeve. *Flying Saucer Pilgrimage*. Amherst, WI: Amherst Press, 1957.

Robertson, David G. *UFOs, Conspiracy Theories and the New Age*. New York, NY: Bloomsbury Academic, 2016.

Rojas, Alejandro. "Remote Controlled UFO Invasion: RC Aircraft Mistaken for UFOs." In *Open Minds*. Tempe, AZ: Open Minds Production, LLC, 2014.

Ronson, Jon. *The Men Who Stare at Goats*. New York, NY: Simon & Schuster, Inc., 2004.

Roseberry, Dinah. *UFO & Alien Management*. Atglen, PA: Schiffer Publishing, Ltd., 2014.

Ross, Hugh, Kenneth Samples, and Mark Clark. *Lights in the Sky & Little Green Men*. Colorado Springs, CO: NavPress, 2002.

Ruppelt, Edward J. *The Report on Unidentified Flying Objects*. Garden City, NY: Doubleday & Company, Inc., 1956.

Sachs, Margaret and Ernest Jahn. *Celestial Passengers: UFOs and Space Travel.* New York, NY: Penguin Books, 1977.

Sacks, Oliver. *Hallucinations*. New York, NY: Random House, Inc., 2013.

Sagan, Carl. *Contact*. New York, NY: Pocket Books, 1985.

Sagan, Carl. *The Cosmic Connection: An Extraterrestrial Perspective*. New York, NY: Dell Publishing Co., Inc., 1973.

Salas, Robert and James Klotz. *Faded Giant*. North Charleston, SC: BookSurge, LLC, 2005.

Sanderson, Ivan T. *Invisible Residents: The Reality of Underwater UFOs*. Kempton, IL: Adventures Unlimited Press, 1970, 2005.

Sanderson, Ivan T. *Uninvited Visitors: A Biologist Looks at UFOs*. New York, NY: Cowles, 1967.

Saunders, David R. and R. Roger Harkins. *UFOs? Yes! Where the Condon Committee Went Wrong*. New York, NY: Signet, 1968.

Schulzetenberg, Mark. *Our Lady Comes to Fátima*. St. Paul, MN: The Leaflet Missal Company, 1987.

Scully, Frank. *Behind the Flying Saucers*. New York, NY: Henry Holt and Company, 1950.

Smith, Warren. *UFO Trek*. New York, NY: Zebra, 1976.

Soriano, Frank and James Bouck. *UFOs Above the Law*. Atglen, PA: Schiffer Publishing Ltd., 2011.

Spencer, John and Hilary Evans, eds. *Phenomenon: Forty Years of Flying Saucers*. New York, NY: Avon, 1988.

Sprague, Ryan. "One by One They Fall." In *Open Minds*. Tempe, AZ: Open Minds Production, LLC, 2014.

Stanton, L. Jerome. *Flying Saucers: Hoax or Reality?* New York, NY: Belmont Books, 1966.

Steiger, Brad. *Alien Meetings*. New York, NY: Ace Books, 1978.

Steiger, Brad. *The Fellowship: Spiritual Contact Between Humans and Outer Space Beings*. New York, NY: Ivy Books, 1988.

Steiger, Brad. *Project Blue Book*. New York, NY: Ballantine Books, 1976.

Steiger, Brad, Alfred Bielek, and Sherry Hanson Steiger. *The Philadelphia Experiment & Other UFO Conspiracies*. New Brunswick, NJ: Inner Light Publications, 1990.

Steiger, Brad and Francie Steiger. *The Star People*. New York, NY: Berkley Books, 1981.

Steiger, Brad and Sherry Hansen Steiger. *The UFO Abductors*. New York, NY: Berkley Books, 1988.

Steiger, Brad and Joan Whritenour. *Flying Saucer Invasion Target—Earth*. New York, NY: Award Books, 1969.

Steiger, Brad and Joan Whritenour. *New UFO Breakthrough*. New York, NY: Award Books, 1968.

Strieber, Whitley. *Alien Hunter: Underworld*. New York, NY: Tor, 2014.

Strieber, Whitley. *Breakthrough: The Next Step*. New York, NY: HarperPaperbacks, 1995.

Strieber, Whitley. *Communion*. New York, NY: HarperCollinsPublishers, 1987.

Strieber, Whitley. *Confirmation: The Hard Evidence of Aliens Among Us*. New York, NY: St. Martin's Press, 1998.

Strieber, Whitley. *The Grays*. New York, NY: Tor, 2006.

Strieber, Whitley. *Majestic*. New York, NY: Berkeley Books, 1989.

Strieber, Whitley. *The Secret School: Preparation for Contact*. New York, NY: HarperPaperbacks, 1997.

Strieber, Whitley. *Solving the Communion Enigma*. New York, NY: Penguin Group Inc., 2011.

Strieber, Whitley. *Transformation: The Breakthrough*. New York, NY: William Morrow, 1988.

Strieber, Whitley and Jeffrey J. Kripal. *The Super Natural: A New Vision of the Unexplained*. New York, NY: Penguin Random House, 2016.

Stringfield, Leonard H. *Situation Red: The UFO Siege!* New York, NY: Fawcett Crest, 1977.

Tonnies, Mac. *The Cryptoterrestrials*. San Antonio, TX: Anomalist Books, 2010.

Trench, Brinsley Le Poer. *The Flying Saucer Story*. New York, NY: Ace Books, 1966.

Trench, Brinsley Le Poer. *Mysterious Visitors: The UFO Story.* New York, NY: Stein and Day, 1971.

Trench, Brinsley Le Poer. *Secret of the Ages: UFO's from Inside the Earth.* New York, NY: Pinnacle Books, 1974.

Turner, Karla. *Into the Fringe: A True Story of Alien Abduction.* New York, NY: The Berkeley Publishing Group, 1992.

Turner, Karla. *Taken: Inside the Alien-Human Agenda.* Tallahassee, FL: Rose Printing Company, Inc., 1994.

Turner, Karla and Ted Rice. *Masquerade of Angels.* Roland, AR: Kelt Works, 1994.

Vallee, Jacque. *Anatomy of a Phenomenon: The Detailed and Unbiased Report of UFOs*. New York, NY: Ace Books, Inc., 1965.

Vallee, Jacque. *Dimensions: A Casebook of Alien Contact.* New York, NY: Ballantine Books, 1988.

Vallee, Jacque. *Passport to Magonia: From Folklore to Flying Saucers.* Chicago, IL: Henry Regnery Company, 1969.

Vallee, Jacques. *Revelations: Alien Contact and Human Deception.* New York, NY: Ballantine Books, 1991.

Vallee, Jacque. *UFO Chronicles of the Soviet Union: A Cosmic Samizdat.* New York, NY: Ballantine Books, 1992.

Vallee, Jacque and Janine Vallee. *The UFO Enigma: Challenge to Science.* New York, NY: Ballantine Books, 1966.

Walters, Ed and Francis Walters. *UFO Abductions in Gulf Breeze*. New York, NY: Avon Books, 1994.

Walton, Travis. *The Walton Experience.* New York, NY: Berkley Medallion, 1978.

Weldon, John and Zola Levitt. *UFOs: What on Earth is Happening?* New York, NY: Bantam Books, 1975.

White, Dale. *Is Something Up There?* New York, NY: Scholastic Book Services, 1968.

Wilkins, Harold T. *Flying Saucers on the Attack.* New York, NY: Citadel Press, 1954.

Wilkins, Harold T. *Flying Saucers Uncensored.* New York, NY: Pyramid Books, 1955.

Williamson, George Hunt. *Other Tongues, Other Flesh.* London: Neville Spearman, 1965.

Williamson, George Hunt. *Road in the Sky.* London, UK: Futura Publications, Ltd., 1975.

Wilson, Dr. Clifford. *The Alien Agenda.* New York, NY: Signet, 1988.

Wilson, Dr. Clifford. *UFOs . . . and Their Mission Impossible.* New York, NY: Signet, 1974.

Wilson, Don. *Secrets of Our Spaceship Moon.* New York, NY: Dell, 1979.

Wright, Susan. *UFO Headquarters: Investigations on Current Extraterrestrial Activity.* New York, NY: St. Martin's Paperbacks, 1998.

Yenne, Bill. *The Evergreen Story.* San Francisco, CA: AGS BookWorks, Inc., 2008.

Yenne, Bill. *U.F.O. Evaluating the Evidence*. New York, NY: Smithmark Publishers, 1997.

Young, Mort. *UFO: Top Secret.* New York, NY: Essandess Special Editions, 1967.

Yurdozo, Farah. *Love in an Alien Purgatory: The Life and Fantastic Art of David Huggins*. San Antonio, TX: Anomalist Books, 2009.

Zinsstag, Lou and Timothy Good. *George Adamski: The Untold Story.* Beckenham, Kent, England, UK: CETI Publications, 1983.

Zullo, Allan. *We're Here: True Tales of Alien Encounters*. New York, NY: Scholastic Inc., 1995.

Index

52